HOW TO PARENT
SO CHILDREN WILL LEARN

Sylvia B. Rimm, Ph.D.

Illustrated by
Katherine Raue Maas

Apple Publishing Company
W6050 Apple Road
Watertown, WI 53094

Library of Congress Cataloging in Publication Data

Rimm, Sylvia B.
How To Parent So Children Will Learn

    Bibliography: p.
    1. Education 2. Parenting

Printed and bound in the United States of America.

Illustrations: Katherine Raue Maas

ISBN No. 0-937891-02-9
Library of Congress Catalogue Card No. 89-84190

This book is dedicated to my parents,

Reva and Harry Barkan

To my mom who modeled for me, that "women can do everything."

To my dad who affectionately advised me that when it rained, I could walk between the drops.

I thank my parents for courageously immigrating to the United States, thus, providing me with this country's opportunities so that I could learn.

CONTENTS

Preface

Parents often wonder why some children enjoy school, love learning and achieve so well in the classroom, while other children, who are equally capable, are so negative about school, avoid learning and underachieve. They may find themselves baffled because the bright, happy child they used to know has "shut down" to learning. Potentially intelligent children don't automatically fulfill their early promise.

Schools are often blamed for children's problems. Indeed, schools and teachers do make a major difference in encouraging children's learning. However, you as parents, can have a dramatic positive impact on your children's education. Positive school experiences increase the likelihood of positive life experiences. Education continues to provide the most effective path to upward mobility and success.

Dr. Spock's advice to millions of parents was a message to have confidence in themselves. He assured them that they could rely on their "parenting instincts."

Relying on one's instincts may result in reasonably effective parenting for those who were brought up in families of origin where there was good parenting, but many parents aren't so sure that they were parented well. They may, in their efforts to change, "instinctively" parent at the opposite extreme. Since they remember mainly their own adolescence, they assume that their parents treated them similarly when they were young children. Their selective memories may thus cause them to "instinctively" parent their own children poorly. Many parents attempt to parent by the Golden Rule: Do unto others as you would have them do unto you. This important rule could not have been intended for parenting. It may trap them into treating children like adults.

All in all, moms and dads seem to find themselves bewildered about the parenting process. They know for sure that they can't love their children too much, but most other parenting guidelines and books leave them floundering in confusion and contradiction. Yet there are highly predictable home and school environments that do guide capable children on paths along which they will learn and will feel good about themselves.

Family Achievement Clinic* specializes in working with bright children who aren't performing to their abilities in school. It employs a TRIFOCAL Model to reverse this underachievement. Treatment is focused on the child, the home and the school to help children achieve and feel good about themselves. There are many changes that can be made at home and school that have already been described in earlier books (Rimm, 1986; Rimm, Cornale, Manos, & Behrend, 1989). There are a few main or significant recommendations that I regularly give to parents in our Clinic which have a dramatic impact on children's school learning and achievement experiences. Of the literally thousands of questions I answer regularly for parents, teachers, radio and television audiences, there emerge some basic common sense themes which make significant differences.

*Family Achievement Clinic, 1227 Robruck Drive, Oconomowoc, WI 53066

This book is written to give you those main guidelines which other parents have found so effective in fostering a home environment that encourages their children's love and respect for learning. Hopefully, these guidelines will help you to prevent problems, as well as to solve them. If you parent using these guidelines, it is likely that your children will learn to enjoy learning.

I would like to thank our Clinic children and their parents for sharing their lives with me and providing the feedback to confirm that my parenting recommendations are effective. A special message of appreciation goes to Sharon Lind who persistently reminded me that parents should have this parenting book. I'd like also to indicate my appreciation to Tom Clark and Wisconsin Public Radio for giving me an extensive audience of parents whose questions I answer regularly, thus permitting me to focus on the main practical concerns of most moms and dads. I want to acknowledge as well those parents in my radio, TV and personal audiences who permit me to feel assured that my parenting advice is practical and realistic. Thanks especially to my publications staff, Marilyn Knackert, Barbara Ruder, Gladys Bennett and Marian Carlson for their help in the preparation and proofreading of my book. Finally, my appreciation is extended to the families who reviewed my final manuscript and made suggestions and comments which were so helpful.

Happy parenting. May parenting provide you the joys that it has for my husband and myself!

1

Praise and Power

Children thrive in an environment of being valued and loved. Praise for children's accomplishments encourages them to continue to accomplish and share their achievements with those whom they please. Attention to their smiles, their gurgles, their "patty cakes" and "bye-byes" enhances their communication and their learning. Reading to children, discussing, sharing interests and answering their questions expands their vocabulary, their information and their intelligence. They soon find that their own vocabulary, knowledge and reasoning empower them to capture adult conversation. They have thus learned that intelligence and learning are valued in their home. This is an apparent good beginning to a lifetime of learning. Praise, attention and positive reinforcement are good for children.

Too Much Praise, Too Much of a Good Thing

Some parents who recognize the value of praise, make the assumption that if some praise is good, more praise must be better. Other parents may assume that if they praise their children in extravagant terms, it will build their children's self-concepts even more. In their attempts to build children's confidence, some parents praise too much. Too much praise may cause your children to become praise dependent or "attention

addicted." Too extravagant praise may result in your children feeling extremely pressured because they believe they must live up to those extraordinary and impossible standards. Both are "too much of a good thing."

You may praise your child as a good worker, as bright, creative, kind or attractive. Please don't use terms like brilliant, extraordinary, perfect, stunning, spectacular, genius, best, most beautiful or favorite. The first are qualities they can control by their own efforts. The last may be internalized as impossible goals and are highly competitive. Unless they turn out to be spectacular, brilliant, perfect and beautiful, they may feel frustrated about their inadequacies forever. They may also blame you for putting pressure on them, although you'll wonder where that pressure came from.

A mother shared with me her surprise at her son's frustration with her high expectations for him. She kept reassuring him by telling him that he was already perfect. She thought that would help. It made him feel more and more pressured. He thought she expected him to be perfect. Her words of praise were viewed by her son as her expectations. Reasonable praise feels like reasonable expectations. Extraordinary praise feels like extraordinary expectations.

Don't praise your children for every accomplishment, for every word or drawing or clever piece of knowledge. Permit them to enjoy the inner rewards of learning and creating. Be sure to insist that they work and play alone for a little time each day so that they can feel the fun of learning and so that they don't become dependent on an audience. Children who become attention addicted at home may feel, by comparison, attention deprived at school. They may also feel attention neglected when siblings enter the family with whom

they must share the limelight. Their sense of special-
ness which was dependent on continuous praise may
disappear when they find they must share attention.
The adult attention to the excitement of learning is
displaced by nonresponsive adults or adults who only
respond to behavior problems and negative behaviors.
Children who have been attention addicted may shut
down to school learning when they feel attention
deprived in the classroom.

Some praise may empower children to feel confident
and to love learning. Too much praise may enslave
them to pressure and dependence. Children who have
been told they are the best, believe they must always
be the best. Children who have been admired as perfect
believe that they must be perfect. Perfect and the best
don't live in the real world. Don't imprison your children
with impossible goals in the hope of building their
self-confidence.

Empower Your Child With the Power to Be a Child

When children are small, they require small amounts
of power. As they get older and grow in maturity and
responsibility, they should have expanded power. Don't
treat children as little adults. Give them child, not adult,
choices. Don't consult them in everything or assume
that they can share your adult experiences and feelings. Let them look forward to adult privileges and
power and permit them to gradually earn adult status.

Particular home situations increase the likelihood
that parents may "adultize" children. They include
giftedness, birth order (oldest or only children), single
parenting and divorce. Adultizing confers some benefits, but also provides some serious risks for healthy
development.

5

ADULT POWER BY GIFTEDNESS

I'VE RESEARCHED THE POTENTIAL SCHOOLS WITH YOU MOTHER, AND DESPITE THE HIGH TUITION, PARK RIDGE INDEPENDENT IS THE ONLY SCHOOL WHICH WILL PROVIDE APPROPRIATE CHALLENGE.

Giftedness increases the likelihood of adultizement because very bright children often display advanced vocabulary, reasoning skills and sensitivities that cause parents to assume that they are more mature. They may actually be more mature than their age-mates, but aren't likely to be as mature as they sound. They require the opportunity to play out a reasonable childhood. They are children first, gifted children second.

"Only" children and oldest children are frequently treated like one of the adults in the family. It's reasonably easy for parents to accommodate one child and they frequently do so, sometimes at the expense of the other adult. Thus, these children become accustomed to equal status and sometimes, more than equal power. They may sound exactly like little adults as they "boss" other children or insist on being treated as an equal to their parents.

Single parents and those undergoing divorce frequently choose one child, usually their oldest, as confidant and partner. They may actually view this child as the main purpose of their lives and direct all their efforts toward the emotional sustenance of that child. They may discuss major life issues and even share their bed. They often assure the child that they will always love him or her more than anyone else in the entire world. The closeness and intimacy that they would normally have with a spouse is replaced by their relationship with this favored child. The adultizing of the child may result from the parent's feelings of rejection and vulnerability. Sometimes these parents feel that they must compensate for the insecurity they perceive the children feel because they have only one parent.

The advantages of adultizement to children include the social, intellectual and apparent emotional sophistication which emerges from this close and

enriched experience with their parent. The major disadvantages come from the feelings of insecurity and powerlessness that emerge with too much adult power. They may feel insecure because they simply don't know how to limit themselves. In classroom and peer relationships, where they aren't given adult status, they may feel "put down" or not respected by comparison to the way in which they're regarded at home. They actually feel "depowered" relative to the feelings of being empowered at home (Rimm et. al., 1989).

The most difficult risk is "dethroning." When another sibling is born or the parent remarries, although the child knows he/she should be happy about the new member of the family, he/she may feel irrationally and extraordinarily jealous (Rimm and Lowe, 1988). Dethroned children may exhibit anger or sadness. Their personalities may change so dramatically that parents, teachers and even doctors may assume they're undergoing a clinical depression.

If you adultize children too early, you will find that they want to run your family, their teachers and other students. As in politics, too much power may corrupt. Children who try to "boss" the rest of the world seem obnoxious at best. They may become continuous arguers who argue about everything. When an adult dares to say "no," they argue. They believe that if they provide sufficient reason, they are *always* right. They say, "Why would I argue, unless I was right?"

Those arguing children no longer can see merit in any opinion but their own. As they trap you into the battles you promised yourself you would handle rationally, you find yourself losing your temper again. How did this happen? Sometimes you feel as if you'd like to kick them. How can that ten-year-old believe he or she can run the entire family? Does this child have no humility at all?

Teachers and parents are offended by such powerful children. They try to "put them in their places." Soon, adults respond to these dictatorial, offensive children with a big "no" permanently engraved on their foreheads. The children make requests. Adults say no. Adults stop listening. "No, no, no. Go away," they say. "Unfair," the children say. Undaunted, they argue.

Directions of Power

Children may exhibit too much power in either dependent or dominant directions or both. Dominant power is easily identified in aggressive children who want to monopolize attention or children who argue as described earlier. They are readily viewed as too powerful.

Dependent children who manipulate their adult world in ways that say "take care of me, feel sorry for me, make things easier, help me, protect me or shelter me," are not usually recognized as powerful. Although their power may result from feelings of powerlessness and their words and body language suggest that they are powerless, their requests for help attract and maintain much more adult attention, protection and assistance than they require. Early adult caretakers did too much for these dependent children. They were helped and protected so much that they're in the habit of "pushing adult buttons" for assistance. They don't take initiative. Instead they ask for more and more help at home and in school. Since many of the adults in their environments are kind and caring and since their symptoms of power (tears and feel-sorry-for-me words) are very persuasive, parents and teachers continue to protect them and unintentionally steal from them their opportunities to cope with challenge. As a result, these children don't develop sufficient self-confidence to build the independent power that fosters achievement and accomplishment. Instead, their tenuous control is directed at the covert (hidden) manipulation of adults. They hardly ever manipulate intentionally. However, they do manipulate effectively and extensively.

The children in the inner circle in Figure 1.1 are achievers. They've internalized a sense of the relationship between efforts and outcomes. That is, they persevere because they recognize that their efforts make a difference. They know how to cope with competition. They love to win, but when they lose or experience a failure, they don't give up. Instead, they try again. They don't view themselves as failures but only see the experience as unsuccessful and learn from it. No children (or adults) remain in the inner circle at all times. For achieving children, however, the inner circle represents their predominant behavior. Outside the circle are prototypical children which represent characteristics of Underachievement Syndrome. These children have learned avoidance and defensive behaviors to protect their fragile self-concepts because they fear taking the risk of making the efforts which might only lead to less-than-perfect performance.

The children on the left are those who've learned to manipulate adults in their environment in dependent ways. Their words and body language say, "Take care of me, protect me, this is too hard, feel sorry for me, I need help." Adults in these children's lives accidentally provide more protection and help than the children need. As a result these children get so much help from others that they lose self-confidence. They do less and parents and teachers expect less. They finally slip between the cracks. Neither they nor their parents or teachers recognize the capabilities which were exhibited when they were younger.

13

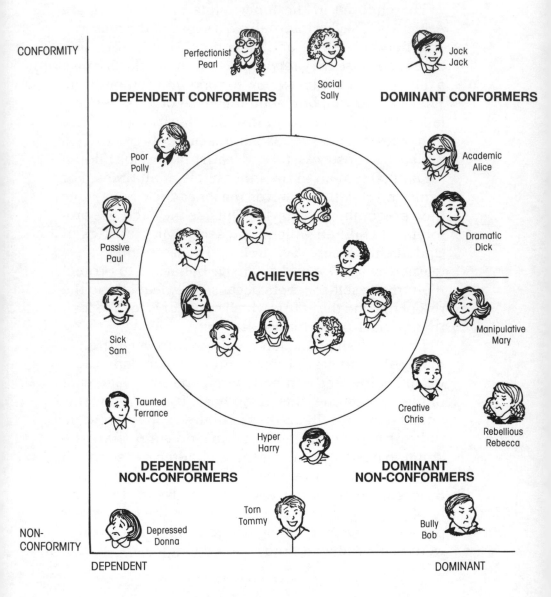

Figure 1

THE INNER CIRCLE OF ACHIEVERS

CONFORMITY

Perfectionist Pearl

Social Sally

Jock Jack

DEPENDENT CONFORMERS

DOMINANT CONFORMERS

Poor Polly

Academic Alice

Passive Paul

Dramatic Dick

ACHIEVERS

Sick Sam

Manipulative Mary

Taunted Terrance

Creative Chris

Rebellious Rebecca

Hyper Harry

DEPENDENT NON-CONFORMERS

DOMINANT NON-CONFORMERS

Torn Tommy

Bully Bob

NON-CONFORMITY

Depressed Donna

DEPENDENT

DOMINANT

14

On the right side of the circle are the dominant children. These children only select activities where they feel confident they'll be winners. They tend to believe that they know best about almost everything. Their manipulations trap parents and teachers into arguments. The adults attempt to be fair and rational. The dominant children attempt to win because they believe they're always right. If the children lose, they consider the adults to be their enemies. Once the adults are established as enemies, they use that enmity as an excuse for not doing their work or taking their responsibilities. Gradually, the children increase their list of adult enemies. These youth lose confidence in themselves because it's based precariously on their successful manipulation of parents and teachers. Adults tire of being manipulated and respond negatively. The dominant children complain that adults don't like them, and indeed, a negative atmosphere becomes pervasive.

The difference between the upper and lower quadrants in the Figure is the degree of and visibility of these children's problems. Children in the upper quadrants have minor problems which can often be prevented from escalating. However, if upper quadrant children continue in their patterns, they will be likely to move into lower quadrants. Many of the dependent children will, by adolescence, change to dominant or mixed dependent/dominant patterns. There are some children who combine both dependent and dominant characteristics from the start.

Neither of the two extremes, dependent or dominant power, appear to cause major problems at home during the preschool years. Parents often become accustomed to dependency or dominance. They may label their dependent child as somewhat immature, and assume that the child will outgrow the problem. They may even acknowledge that their too domineering child seems a little bit "spoiled." They have reasonable confidence, however, that their child's problems will be resolved by his or her entrance to school. They expect that teachers and the school structure will help their too powerful child adjust.

Dependent and dominant children have practiced these control patterns for several years before they enter school. It feels to them that these behaviors work well and they know no others. They carry them into the classroom and expect to relate to teachers and peers in the same powerful directions. Teachers may be effective in changing some of the children's ways of relating. However, the more extreme the dependency or dominance is, the more difficult it will be to modify. Furthermore, the dependency pattern is often masked as insecurity, immaturity, hyperactivity or even a learning disability. The dominant pattern sometimes may not show itself in the early elementary grades since the child may feel fulfilled by the excitement and power of school achievement. Dominance may also be exhibited as giftedness or creativity, or not-so-positively, as a discipline problem.

Even if some teachers manage these children well in school, the dependent or dominant patterns may continue to be reinforced at home. If so, they'll surely surface in later years. These dependent and dominant children are likely to become underachievers because their self-confidence is built on manipulating others instead of on their own accomplishments.

In granting children power, we must give them sufficient freedom and power to provide them with the courage for intellectual risk taking. However, we should also teach sufficient humility so that they recognize that their views of the world are not the only correct ones. We must empower them sufficiently to study, learn, question, persevere, challenge and discuss but not grant them so much power that they infringe on parents' and teachers' fragile authority for guiding them.

On May 25, 1989, I sat with thousands of parents and family members at the commencement ceremony of the Johns Hopkins University (our son, David, was among the graduates). Dr. Steven Muller, President of the University, provided a farewell to the audience that seemed to bear an uncanny resemblance to the message about power and freedom which I regularly give to parents. I've excerpted the lines which seem appropriate for your children. As you read it, please substitute *our family* for this University or Johns Hopkins University.

> . . . As we congratulate you on your academic attainments and wish you well, it also seems more timely than ever to remind you . . . that you have received here a great blessing, and that therefore you bear as well a great responsibility. Whatever your field of study, you have been blessed by academic freedom in all fullness. "Veritas Vos Liberabit" — "The Truth Shall Make You Free" — is the motto of this university. . .

> . . . Let me point out as well that you here today are privileged already to be citizens of the information society; that your education at Johns Hopkins qualifies you for leadership; that the freedom of your education is the world's envy; and that the information technology of tomorrow will make today's mere beginnings look like child's play.

17

But let me also remind you that knowledge alone is not wisdom; that information is a means, not an end; that the object of free inquiry is truth, not profit; **that freedom without responsibility is animal anarchy**...

...Today we celebrate with you your intelligence and your academic achievements ...And at Johns Hopkins we invest you with a special trust and mission: to continue your search for truth; to cherish freedom as the only way to truth; to live by the truth that human beings who seek to be free of a master must then **be fully masters of themselves**...

Dr. Muller's message to those graduates can guide you in providing the freedom which matches children's capabilities for responsibility so that your family will not resemble "animal anarchy" and so that they may grow to be "masters of themselves."

The Dependent Pattern - Facilitating Independent Power

As parents, be sensitive to not doing for your children what they can do for themselves or they can't build self-confidence. If you wonder why it is that these powerful dependent children don't have self-confidence, think of the ways in which you've built your own personal self-confidence. You didn't build confidence by accomplishing easy tasks which you knew other people could also accomplish easily. It's when you approached a challenge, but you took the risk of attempting it and found you could accomplish something that you never believed you could before, that you climbed one small step up the ladder of self-confidence. You took one small step at a time and built your personal self-confidence. In the same way, your children must

19

earn their confidence one small step at a time. No matter how many times you tell them how bright or capable they are, you can't anoint them with self-confidence. Unfortunately, they must struggle to earn it. If, in the name of kindness, you steal their struggle, you'll find that you've also stolen that illusive self-confidence.

An example of a dependent manipulation was shared with me by the mother of a fourth-grade, physically handicapped child.

Each morning Alex's mother dressed him to be ready for school. She was a teacher and had to get to work on time. Alex was very slow. She came to hear my talk and I pointed out how dependent children are prevented from building self-confidence. She described her son's situation to me and agreed that he had very little confidence. I asked if he was capable of dressing himself and she indicated that he was. I pointed out to her that if he was capable and wasn't dressing himself that he couldn't have self-confidence.

Alex's mother resolved to change the pattern by insisting that he dress himself independently. She chose a Saturday for fear of attempting the new struggle on a work day. She told Alex that from now on she expected him to dress himself. He protested. She insisted. She said he couldn't leave his room until he had dressed himself. He eyed her imploringly and proceeded to cry. She left, indicating she would come back *only* after he was dressed.

Alex's sobs, cries, screams and his desperation were hard for her to listen to so she retreated to the laundry room where she hoped the dryer noise would muffle his cries.

As she folded laundry, she kept repeating, "I hate Sylvia Rimm, I hate Sylvia Rimm, I hate Sylvia Rimm." Finally, after two hours, Alex had successfully dressed himself. On Sunday, Alex dressed in half an hour. There wasn't any crying or screaming, just the independent dressing. By Monday, Alex dressed in ten minutes. Thus began Alex's requests for new challenges. His confidence grew. His relationship with his mother became more positive and, furthermore, even his stepfather acknowledged that he was beginning to like this young man.

Dominant Children and the V of Love

Children should have choices from early on. You, as parents, are responsible for providing and limiting those choices. Jim Fay may be the world's most creative leader on how to provide choices (Fay, 1983, 1988a, 1988b). He suggests that by "the time youngsters can sit in a high chair and spit beets," they can learn from choices (Fay, 1989). If the baby spits out his/her food, the baby is making the choice not to eat. Calm removal from the high chair until the next meal makes the consequence clear.

Children can learn early to choose their own clothes from the appropriate group presented by a parent. They should not be permitted to choose from whatever they want. For example, for school they may choose from their school clothes, but not from their play clothes. Parents provide the limits to their choices. They choose to dress *themselves* if they're going to get to school dressed (see Morning Routine, Chapter 3). They don't choose whether or not to go to school. The number and variety of choices increases with their increased maturity and responsibility.

You're in charge of your children. Children feel secure following their parents' leadership provided they have become accustomed to that mode. Although they're likely to "push limits" sporadically to determine the extent of their freedom, they'll respect the word "no" when it's given firmly and fairly. Children who haven't learned to accept limits in childhood will certainly not accept them in adolescence.

Visualize the letter "V" as a model for guiding your children's power. When they're very young they begin at the bottom of the "V" with limited freedom and power. As they mature and are able to handle more responsibility, the limiting walls of the "V" spread out giving them continually more freedom while still providing definite limits. During adolescence, as they move to the top of the "V" they become capable of considerable independent decision making and judgment, but should continue to recognize that there remain adult prerogatives in guiding them. They are thus readied for moving out of the "V" into adult independence and personal decision making.

Now reverse that "V" so that it looks like this "Λ". Children brought up at the base of this figure are given too much freedom and wide limits. They become accustomed to independent decision making before they're able to handle their freedom responsibly. As they move toward adolescence, parents become concerned that their children may misuse their freedom. They worry about the dangers that arise in school and community. Cigarettes, alcohol, drugs and promiscuous sex are perceived as threats from which their children must be protected. So they begin to set limits. They take freedoms away. Adolescents who had too much control as children now feel overcontrolled by parents. Their statements echo their feelings of restriction. "My parents are controlling me. They used to treat me like an adult and now they treat me like a child," they complain. They push all limits and oppose and rebel. They feel angry and depressed. They lie and cheat. Worried parents overpunish and narrow the limits further, resulting in even more rebellion. Ugly adolescence makes the formerly happy home into an armed camp. Underachievement is only a small part of the problem. Once freedom is given it isn't easily taken away. The "V" shaped guidance is much smoother and more comfortable for adolescents and parents alike.

Empowering children with adult decision making provides power without wisdom. It leads to formidable and continuing conflicts between children and their parents as they compete for the power that parents give too early and try to recover too late. The resulting adversary mode may force adolescents to rebel too stubbornly, parents to respond too negatively, and both to lose the positive home atmosphere that can be so valuable in educating children.

Why Do We Do It? How Do Children Think?

After you've read about dependent and dominant manipulations which you may have reinforced unintentionally and you identify that your children have too much dependent or dominant power, you'll find yourself wondering why you responded to these manipulations in the first place. The answer is simple, but complex. Most good, loving parents project their own feelings into their children. You try to read your children's feelings by thinking about how you would feel under similar circumstances. You remember the Golden Rule, to "do unto others as you would have them do unto you." You then reason with your children

24

as *you* would wish to be reasoned with. You comfort them as you would wish to be comforted. You listen to what they are saying and try to respond to their requests in the same way in which you would wish that your friends would listen and respond to you.

Now, here's the glitch! Your responses are based on the assumption that they have developed cognitively and morally to your adult level. But they **haven't**. They are still only children. They do not think like adults. They are not yet capable of adult thinking.

Many of you have taken high school or college courses in psychology. You may have learned about Piaget's stages of cognitive development and Kohlberg's stages of moral development (Piaget, 1932; Kohlberg & Gilligan, 1971). You may have memorized those stages and repeated them back on exams. You've even read about their theories in popular magazines. These theories have been researched and they seemed logical as you learned about them.

However, although most people accept Piaget or Kohlberg's findings, they don't generalize the stages of development to the practical business of bringing up kids. Instead, many parents, teachers and counselors treat children like little adults and assume that they're wise and mature enough to emit the words and sentences which tell us their needs. We then use their literal communications as the basis for guiding them. We tend to believe that they always know what they're talking about. Even when they have nothing to say, we coax them to express their feelings. They try to comply and often say what we'd like them to. Once their words are spoken, we have the naive belief that the words explain their feelings. We act on what they say because we believe that they must know what's best for them.

Please reflect for a few moments upon your own childhood. When did you begin your introspective exploration of your personal values and motivations? When did you begin to interpret what made you feel sad or glad? When did you start to understand why you procrastinated or why you didn't? When did you understand the underlying basis for your elations and depressions?

Rarely before late adolescence do young people begin in-depth thinking about their own feelings, thoughts and motivations. For me it was in my sophomore or junior year in high school. There was much more in college. And it went on. And it goes on. As adults we continue to learn about ourselves. We look back at our childhood motivations with a very different insight.

Little kids just respond and repeat back beliefs and opinions. Their cognitive development affects their moral development. In early childhood, Kohlberg tells us that children define right by what is rewarded or punished. Later, right becomes what pleases or displeases the important "others" in their lives. They repeat what they've heard and learned. They combine and reorganize adult ideas and restate them. When we hear the words we've taught them (or someone else has), we respond to them as if the ideas were theirs in the first place. Little kids really need to be little kids until their brain structure and their experiences permit them to grow gradually into adults. Examine the information you have about your children and their environments before you respond to their expressions of feelings. There are many possibilities for the true meanings of what they say (see Inset 1.1). Rarely do they understand their underlying motivations. Listen to the words of your children and interpret them with your adult wisdom.

	INSET 1.1 — HOW DO CHILDREN THINK?	
Children Say	Parents' Usual Response	Alternative Interpretations
I need help.	This must be too hard. I should help.	It may actually be too difficult and my child may need help or...
		My child may be afraid to try.
		My child is accustomed to being helped too much.
		My child avoids anything unfamiliar.
		My child may prefer to play with friends.
My teacher doesn't like me.	The teacher has probably said something to hurt my child's feelings.	Perhaps the teacher has, or...
		My child may not be center of attention in this class.
		The teacher may be challenging my child.
		The teacher may have corrected my child.
		The teacher may not praise as much as my child is accustomed to.
The kids are picking on me.	The playground supervisor should be protecting my child.	Maybe the supervisor should or...
		One child said something unpleasant.
		My child wasn't chosen for the team first.
		Children are retaliating for my child's aggressive behavior.
		Kids are picking on lots of other kids too.

INSET 1.1 — HOW DO CHILDREN THINK? (continued)		
I feel sad.	Something terrible must have happened that my child can't talk about.	Possibly true or. . . My child did poorly on a test. My child feels bored. My child didn't get a toy that was wanted. My child got in trouble in school. A friend couldn't come to play.
I want to cure cancer and help the world.	My child is so sensitive, caring and smart. Maybe he/she will cure cancer.	My child may be caring and smart or. . . My child knows that people smile and hug when he/she talks about curing the world. Grandma just died of cancer and he/she misses her. People tell my child that he/she is smart enough to cure cancer and that makes my child feel smart.
School is boring.	I wish schools were arranged to challenge bright children.	There may not be enough challenge or. . . There may be too much challenge. There may be a lot of written work. The teacher may not be a stand-up comedian. The child may prefer recess or lunch.

Take-Charge Techniques for Parents

There are a few sure techniques that you may use that will help you to lead your children so that they may feel guided and secure. As your children grow, you'll be able to add to their choices and their power. **Please increase their power slowly.** Remember that once power is given, it's not easily taken away. Since my techniques may feel depowering for some too powerful children, be prepared for some anger, tantrums or temporary depression. The power we're taking from them is manipulative power. In the long run, they'll be better off without it. The power they'll earn and learn is positive personal power. It will strengthen them and help them to build confidence. The two kinds of power don't fit well together. We must remove the first to give the second. It will work. Be patient and calm.

Rewards and Punishments. The oldest tools for teaching are rewards and punishments. Kohlberg explains that early stages of morality are shaped by adult rewards and punishments (Kohlberg & Gilligan, 1971). Although they've been used by adults to guide children's learning forever, new theories and new research serve to implement and sometimes contradict the common-sense approaches of the past. The purpose for the use of rewards and punishments is children's learning — learning to learn, learning to live.

A target provides a model for the continuum and variety of rewards and punishments. The bull's-eye of that target represents intrinsic rewards and punishments. They come from the satisfaction or dissatisfaction of producing or not producing quality work. Intrinsic satisfaction comes when children develop interests. The enthusiasm and excitement of learning experiences provide intrinsic rewards. Your goal is to encourage many bull's-eye rewards for your children's

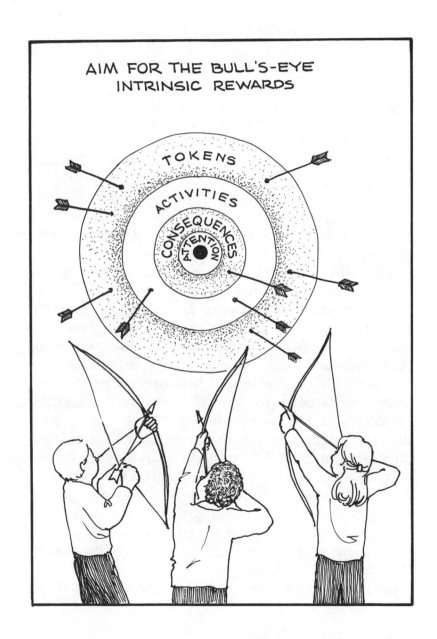

AIM FOR THE BULL'S-EYE
INTRINSIC REWARDS

TOKENS
ACTIVITIES
CONSEQUENCES
ATTENTION

31

learning experiences. Observe a one-year-old dropping blocks into a container, dumping them, then repeating the activity to see intrinsic rewards. Notice a high school artist absorbed for hours in a watercolor painting to see intrinsic rewards.

As in target practice, the bull's-eye is hardest to hit. The wider circles that surround the bull's-eye are easier. They're more frequently used by parents. Outside of the bull's-eye circle is a somewhat larger circle which provides the second best tools for rewarding and punishing children. These rewards are the attention of parents, teachers and close family members. Attention is very effective in teaching children to be learners, workers and thinkers. When important adults indicate that they're pleased with children's performances, their praise serves as a reward. Their disappointment feels like a punishment.

The third circle, the natural, positive or negative consequences of an activity, provides the next most effective rewards and punishments. (You may prefer to interchange circles two and three. They are close in importance.) Good grades are a consequence for children's hard work. Poor grades are a consequence for lack of effort. Children who dress themselves independently come to school feeling better than the children who are nagged before school. The first are experiencing positive consequences; the latter, negative consequences. Children who start fights suffer the consequence of starting those fights. Other children will fight back or say mean things to them. Consequences serve to automatically reward or punish children in their learning experiences.

Sometimes the consequence of an activity doesn't fit the experience. It may, therefore, provide inappropriate learning. Your child may not have studied and received an *A* on the test anyway. That child may believe that school is easy and study is unimportant. You may not be able to control those inappropriate circumstances. Other times, you may be able to reorganize the order of learning experiences to shape consequences which will automatically reinforce your children (like in the Morning and Homework Routines in Chapter 3.)

The personal attention of important adults and natural consequences are preferable to the two broad outer reward and punishment rings of the target. Ring four uses activities as a reward for children's learning performance and withdrawal of activities as a punishment. Parents use the withdrawal or punishment component of activities more frequently than the reward component. Activity punishments are often overused. Parents frequently take away activities for long periods of time. The term used for withdrawing social activities is usually "grounding." Some parents "ground" for a day or two, others "ground" for a week or two and some others "ground for life." When children are grounded for life, they can do almost anything and they feel angry enough to try almost anything. They want to get even by "punishing parents back."

The final largest ring of the circle is material rewards and punishments which may include stickers, baseball cards, stars, money, gifts, etc. These are referred to as token reinforcements and are probably used most frequently of all. Token reinforcements are effective reinforcements for short-term purposes. However, they tend to be overused. Children may learn to negotiate tokens or become dependent on their use. Token rewards are most effective when they're used temporarily as a bridge to the inner circles of the target.

Overuse of material rewards may teach children to manipulate adults for tokens. For example, one young man who was getting money for his work completion in school stopped doing his work. He asked for an increase in money to return to this earlier schoolwork completion. Sometimes children who have been paid for doing home chores will ask for a higher payment for doing the same chores. They may refuse to do any chores unless they're paid. These are negative side effects of overuse of token reinforcements.

Our Clinic experiences do support the effectiveness of token rewards. We use them frequently to initiate a study or chore schedule. However, we emphasize to children that we're using them temporarily. We want to help children move toward higher-level reward systems like improved grades (consequences), improved feelings between family members (positive attention), and most of all, improved self-confidence (intrinsic). In that way, the children understand the plan and the goal of the token rewards. They recognize them as a temporary means of helping them change bad habits.

The two outer circles of our target are used most often by many parents. As you gain expertise in parenting, you'll find yourself using the three inner circles more frequently.

In summary, rewards and punishments are effective tools for teaching children. Always try to reward as close to the bull's-eye as possible. The entire target is certainly acceptable as long as you recognize that the outer circles are bridges to bull's-eye learning. Most important, don't overreward or overpunish. If you do, it's likely that your children will rarely reach bull's-eye learning.

Overpunishment and Opposition. I don't know of a single achieving child who was inspired toward learning through punishment. Yet, punishment is so frequently and ineffectively used by parents that you might wonder why you find yourself expecting to motivate your children by punishment. Parents continue to use punishments because, at first, they seem to work. Children stop their bad behavior temporarily. However, if parents overuse punishments, there are two side effects. One is that in order to prevent the problem behaviors you'll find that you'll have to use more and bigger punishments, for example, longer and longer "groundings." You'll soon run out of controls that will punish sufficiently to stop all the bad behaviors. The second is that children who are punished so much resent their parents and want to get "even" as in this quotation by one college freshman:

> "My parents punished me, I punished them back. My parents punished me, I punished them back. You would have thought that I'd have realized that since their punishments didn't work, why would mine?"

Nevertheless, that sequence of punishing and counterpunishing is common. It heightens the oppositionality and increases negativism in your family. Soon everyone seems to be punishing everyone else and there's an atmosphere of pervasive anger and "getting even."

If you're in the habit of overpunishing, you are probably also in the habit of shortening or removing these punishments afterwards. That essentially teaches your children that you are all sound and fury, but empty power. They learn to fear you and to manipulate you. You provide the model for anger and the practice for

```
┌──────────────────────────────────────────────────────┐
│         INSET 1.2 — GUIDELINES FOR PUNISHMENT          │
│                                                        │
│  1. Punish calmly.                                     │
│                                                        │
│  2. Punish briefly. Ten minutes, one day, one evening  │
│     are usually sufficient.                            │
│                                                        │
│  3. When you take away something like bicycle,         │
│     telephone, etc., don't expect children to tell you │
│     you're right. They usually say, "I don't care" or  │
│     "that's not fair." They do care.                   │
│                                                        │
│  4. Spanking more than once rarely works.              │
│                                                        │
│  5. If you're very angry, for little children, use     │
│     time-out. For older children, tell them you're     │
│     disappointed and you will give some thought to the │
│     appropriate punishment. (A little healthy fear     │
│     while they're waiting will be effective, and time  │
│     to think about it will keep you more rational.)    │
│                                                        │
│  6. Once your punishment is given, don't take it away. │
│                                                        │
│  7. Be consistent and firm.                            │
│                                                        │
│  8. Don't keep adding additional punishments. That     │
│     only in-creases the resentment.                    │
└──────────────────────────────────────────────────────┘
```

manipulation. You do all of this because you love your children so much and want so much for them to do well, but feel so frustrated at them because they refuse to follow your good advice. You feel powerless. Inset 1.2 gives you some guidelines to use for punishments.

Positive Messages. Positive statements about expectations increase the likelihood that your children will try to carry them through.

For example, if children haven't been efficient in doing homework, some consequences that you may decide to establish are that after homework is done, the family will play some games or watch television or read some stories or have some popcorn (see Chapter 3). These are positive activity rewards for their efficient homework completion. The punishment for children who don't complete their homework would be to not participate in those activities. When you state the expectation to your children, the negative is obvious and will only establish a battling attitude. To state your expectations positively you would say:

"I hope you can finish your homework and do a good job so we can have time to play checkers or Scrabble at 7:00. I'll be looking forward to it."

That statement fosters the child's partnership in work and play. Saying it in a negative way, "If you don't get your homework done, you can't play Scrabble with us," provides the same information. However, the negative statement is likely to make children angry. It may prevent them from wanting to finish their work. They'll feel as if they're losing an argument. Many, many parents emphasize the negative and threaten their children regularly. Continuous threats prevent children from feeling trusted and good about themselves.

Don't be too hard on yourself if every once in awhile you find you're being negative. The frustrations and pressures of parenting may cause all parents to find themselves acting more negatively than they'd like to, occasionally. Be positive as much as you can. Positive environments increase the likelihood of positive children. However, negative slips are human.

Reasoning and Talk. All of us would like to be rational parents and would like our children to be reasonable too. You should teach expected behaviors and explain reasons for those expectations. Part of teaching children appropriate learning behaviors involves explaining to them the reasons why they're expected to accomplish a task or carry through a responsibility. However, keep your discussions brief. Active little children hardly ever hear the whole story anyway. They "turn you off" after your first two or three

38

sentences. Beyond that, your voice becomes a mere nagging background. If you make your statements brief, you'll be more likely to communicate appropriately. You'll also prevent teaching children to do the continuous arguing that makes them into power strugglers.

Overemotional Responses. Many parents are screamers. Mothers and fathers who come to my Clinic sometimes claim they tie for "best (or worst) screamer." However, when fathers scream, mothers tend to believe that fathers scream louder than they do. Mothers often blame screaming fathers for destroying children's self-concepts. Fathers, who hear mothers scream, often complain that mothers are out of control and sometimes criticize their spouses in front of their children.

When you scream at your children, it means that you're feeling powerless to do anything about their behaviors. If you're a continuous screamer, be sure to learn to use the time-out and arguing techniques which follow. If used effectively, these techniques should reduce your screaming to minimal amounts. Remember that when you lose your temper, you're out of control. Your children sense that and recognize that you can't manage them. The result is that the balance of power has shifted. They're in control of you. It makes your children feel insecure when they can "step on" wimpy parents. **Stay calm and in charge.**

Setting Limits by Time-Out. Some children seem too powerful from infancy. Although they are fed, "watered" and loved, they're not contented. By age two, some parents tell me that their children are controlling them and that they find themselves yelling, screaming and acting in irrational ways that they never envisioned for parenthood.

40

"I ask him to sit in the corner and he won't."

"I put her in her room and she comes out."

"I tell him he must eat his vegetables. He eats them and throws them up right at the table."

"I can't control her unless I cry in desperation. Then she stops and puts her arm around me and comforts me."

These parents can hardly believe they have given birth to such misbehaving "monsters." The children have somehow discovered that they're in charge of their caretakers; they have a premature and very severe case of adult power. However, there is great hope when discovered early. *You can take charge and you must.*

In the preschool years, there does appear to be an almost magic solution to regaining control of your children that is 100% effective to date. It's also effective with many children up to age nine or ten. Beyond that, it works with some but not with others. It's not intended for adolescents. If you follow the cookbook recipe for "time-out" explained in Inset 1.3, your children will become much calmer, will obey most of your requests and won't behave as obnoxious little brats. You'll be in control of your children and you'll be a much more confident parent. As long as you maintain that positive control and don't regress to the powerless level of screaming and impossible threats, your children won't return to the insecurities of continuously pushing limits. The change will be dramatic.

INSET 1.3 — RECIPE FOR SUCCESSFUL TIME-OUTS (FOLLOW EXACTLY)

1. All adults and older siblings must follow all rules.

2. One adult tells the child briefly (2 sentences or less) that the consequence for specific enumerated naughty behaviors will be to stay in his/her room for ten minutes of quiet with the door closed.

3. The naughty behaviors should be specified. Don't select all, just the worst (e.g., hitting, temper tantrums, talking back to parents).

4. If the child is likely to open the door when it's closed, arrange it so the door can be locked from the outside. Door handles may be reversed or a latch can be used. One parent suggested looping a rope from one door handle to another door handle. For most powerful children some kind of lock is required, at least initially.

5. For the first and every time the child misbehaves in the stated way, the child should be escorted to the room without the parent losing his/her temper and without giving any further explanation beyond one sentence (e.g., "Since you used bad language, you'll stay in your room for ten quiet minutes".)

6. If the child slams the door, loses his or her temper, bangs on walls, throws toys, screams, shouts or talks, there is to be absolutely no response from anyone. Expect the first few times to be terrible. Remember, absolutely NO response from anyone.

7. Set the timer *only* when the child is quiet (not screaming, tantruming or using disrespectful language — quiet talking to self is fine).

8. After ten minutes, open the door to permit the child to leave. There should be no further explanation or apology or warning or discussion of love. Act as if nothing unusual has happened. **Don't hug!**

9. Repeat as necessary.

10. After one week, only a warning of the closed door should be necessary to prevent the undesirable behavior.

11. You may use "time-out" for warning purposes. Give only one warning. ALWAYS follow through if the child disobeys. REMAIN CALM.

12. Your child will become calmer, appear more secure and be much better behaved.

I know you don't believe me while you're reading this — parents don't believe me in my office either. However, they come to the next visit smiling, convinced, and ready for the next guidelines. The dramatic reversal takes place because you've changed your role from follower to leader. Prior to that, your children were in command and didn't know how to cope with their excessive power. You've just given them clear limits and they feel so much more secure. You're bigger and in charge, and they're now content to follow your secure lead.

Now some of you will feel that Inset 1.3 describes cruel and unusual punishment that you wouldn't want to inflict on your children. You'll want to modify it by explaining to your children afterward how much you love them. If you do, you'll cancel the effect of the time-out by giving them a double message. This time-out is effective only because it completely withdraws attention. If it's punctuated by your words of love, children continue to control you. If you're reading this book, your children know that you love them. It certainly is appropriate to remind them of your love, but not at times when they've misbehaved, and certainly not immediately following their punishment.

Some readers will say, "I've tried time-out. Everyone knows about time-out. It just doesn't work." It's really true that most parents have tried time-out in one form or another, but hardly ever do they follow the exact instructions that are included in Inset 1.3. Some mistakes that parents make in using time-out follow:

1. They permit children to time themselves out in which case they will often slam the door. Parents respond by telling them not to slam the door. In that way children recognize that they're powerful, more powerful than parents and they continue to slam the door.

2. Sometimes parents will make the mistake of talking to children when they call out and ask how much more time they have. Parents may actually start arguing with them. The conversation cancels the effect of withdrawn attention.

3. Some parents are hesitant about locking the door and will stand holding the door closed. The child knows that the parent is holding the door; thus, the power struggle continues.

4. Sometimes after children have thrown things around their room, parents insist that they go back to pick up what they have thrown around. Another power struggle ensues in which case children are in charge of the parent by argument again.

5. Sometimes parents use time-out only after they've yelled and screamed and lost their temper. That's too late. It has to be executed calmly, as if parents are in charge.

Time-out is only effective when it shifts the manipulative power from children to the leadership power of the parents and doesn't draw undue attention to the children's negative behaviors. The withdrawal of power and attention has the effect of setting a definite limit. It makes very, very clear to children that they must stop misbehaving. It's effective for all young children.

Setting Limits for Arguers. If you find yourself feeling trapped by children who want to argue constantly, read this section. You've probably tried to reason and discuss. Before you know it, you find yourself shouting or losing your temper and you're not sure how that ever happened. Sometimes, it's not even clear to you what you're arguing about.

Children who argue incessantly often think of themselves as debaters. They are frequently told by parents that they will make good lawyers. The more you call them "lawyers," the more determined they will be to win all arguments (see Setting Expectations by Referential Speaking, Chapter 4). They pride themselves on their reasoning skills and may extend their debating to teachers and friends.

Although you may sometimes enjoy their critical-thinking ability, you also find yourself feeling pushed, frustrated, manipulated and very negative. When your "debaters" approach, an automatic "no" appears on your forehead. You say no before you even hear their request. "No" feels almost instinctive and, at least, protective. However, arguers don't accept *nos*. They follow you around the room with further convincing discussion until finally, either out of guilt, frustration, desperation or just to deliver yourself from pain, you respond with a negative "all right, yes." You've now, unintentionally, increased their arguing skill by teaching them that if they persevere, you'll surely change your decision. You've also enhanced your negative parent image. Neither were what you intended. You feel trapped.

When you ask a favor of your debating children, oddly enough they also respond with an automatic "no, why do I have to?" You find yourself following them around the room, providing them with a nagging rationale for your request until finally they respond with a negative "all right, if I have to." You wonder why they're so negative when you've been so good to them. They've copied your pattern! Again, you feel trapped.

Children naturally become more skilled in arguing with continued experience. While it's important to encourage critical thinking and discussion, a regular arguing mode is more a power struggle than a discussion. Furthermore, these children are accumulating experiences in always winning power struggles. This is a habit that will make it difficult for them to live or work with others in the future.

The goal of my recommendations is to teach you to encourage thinking and reasoning, but to discourage dominating power struggles. The suggestions permit children the opportunity to respect the experience and intelligence of their parents and teachers, while retaining their own rights as children to think, question and discuss. This isn't an easy balance to maintain. See Inset 1.4:

INSET 1.4 — ANTI-ARGUING INSTRUCTIONS

1. When arguers come at you (they always choose an inconvenient time because they instinctively know you're vulnerable), remind yourself not to say yes or no immediately. Instead, after they've made their request, ask them for their reasons. If you've asked for their reasons, they can never accuse you of not listening.

2. After you've heard their reasons, say, "Let me think about it. I'll get back to you" (in a few minutes or after dinner for a small request; tomorrow or the weekend for a larger one). There are three marvelous benefits to the second step of this arguing process. First, it permits you to continue to be rational (that's what you wanted to be when you accidentally trained your arguers). Secondly, it teaches children to be patient. Since arguers tend to demand "instant gratification," patience is a good quality for them to learn. Third, since arguers are often dominant manipulative children, they know that since you haven't yet responded with either a yes or no, that their being good increases the likelihood of their getting a yes. Therefore, while you are taking time to be rational and while they're learning patience, these lovely dominant children will be at their best behavior. How nice!

---

3. Then think about their request and their reasons. Don't be negatively biased by your feelings or their pushiness. If your answer is yes, smile and be positive and enthusiastic. Dominant arguers rarely see adults smile anymore. If you have a compromise solution, explain that positively and enthusiastically.

4. If your answer is no, and you do have the right and obligation to say no sometimes (even if it's only because you're too tired to drive them someplace), then say no firmly. Include your reason as part of your refusal. Don't change your decision (for at least 90% of the times; you may change 10% of the time for flexibility) and don't engage in further discussions. Don't let them make you feel guilty.

5. Remind them that you've heard their request, you've listened to their reasons, you've taken time to think about them carefully, you've given them your answer and your reason and that the discussion is now over. If they continue arguing, and they're below age ten and not too big, send them to their room (see Time-Out) and lock the door. If they're too big for you to time them out, you go calmly to your room and lock your door. If they beat on your door, ignore them. Relax with a good book or a television program. Finally they'll learn that parents have earned the privilege of saying no. They'll also have learned that they may continue to have the opportunity to remain children. They may not appreciate the latter at the time. However, your home will become a more pleasant and positive place in which to live, and your children will find that you are positive, fair and rational even if you don't always agree with them.

If you have arguers, don't brag to Grandma or a neighbor about your children's creative arguing skills. It will make them more determined than ever to argue until they win. Don't use "I told you so" when your arguers finally give up the battle. The more determined you are to let them know that you're right, the harder it becomes for them to admit their own mistakes. It's better to give no attention to the fact that they've come around to your way of thinking. Time permits them to gracefully acknowledge their mistakes. No one loves to be found

out as "wrong," but insisting that arguers admit their error usually ends in further no-win battles. Occasionally admitting your own flawed reasoning in an argument with someone else, and your approaches to addressing error will model for your children the way to admit mistakes (if you have ever made any). **Humor helps!**

When you lose your temper in an argument, you know you've handled the routine poorly. Go back and read Inset 1.4 again. If you habitually lose your temper, children interpret that as weakness and loss of control. They will style their arguments to last as long as your temper holds out. As they continue to push, you'll find yourself losing your temper more often. Review Inset 1.4 again and again. **It works!**

If you're the other parent, the one who doesn't argue with your children, don't mediate. That's a put-down to your spouse. It's giving children equal power with an adult before they've earned it. Your mediation attempts will increase their arguing behavior with your spouse. After they've developed expertise in arguing with your spouse, they'll generalize that arguing technique and direct it to you. Support your spouse. If you have differences, discuss those without your children knowing about those differences. Under no circumstances should you tell your spouse to control him or herself in front of the children. That will be viewed as conveying adult status to your arguers or child status to your spouse and your children will become openly disrespectful to your spouse (and eventually to you). It's husband/wife sabotage. Parental support for each other is the key to parental leadership (see Chapter 2).

Now that you know how to win the power struggles, read on to learn how to avoid them.

Avoiding Power Struggles. There are two principles that are critical to the issue of power struggles which are important in the relationship between parents and children. Both have been described in the book *Under-achievement Syndrome: Causes and Cures* (Rimm, 1986). The first was stated in Rimm's Law #10, "Avoid confrontations with children unless you can control the outcomes." The second emphasizes the importance of staying in an alliance with your child and refusing to allow yourself to become "the enemy." Those two principles should be your guide in dealing with strong-willed children. You now have several new techniques for limiting children's power. These will help them to respect you.

Many children have already been given so much power that they may involve you in power struggles despite your improved techniques. You will want to learn to change those battles into alliances. This process may call upon the "Pollyanna"* in you as well as requiring your most creative talents. The results are worth it. Here are five examples of how power struggles can be reversed to provide a more positive atmosphere in your home.

Case 1

Brian was nagged regularly each morning before school. He was nagged to wake up, nagged to eat breakfast, nagged to get himself dressed. He depended on his mother's nagging. Every morning represented a power struggle. The morning routine which is described in Chapter 3 was recommended to his mother. After I reviewed the routine with her,

*Pollyanna is a fictional character in a children's book by the same name, authored by Eleanor H. Porter. She always manages to find the bright side to everything.

she went home and began using it immediately. She called me a few days later to complain, in exasperation, that the routine just wasn't working. Since other parents have had so much success with it, I was surprised. When I asked her to describe her experiences, she reviewed the typical steps. Her final statement was, "And then he almost misses the bus."

I reviewed her description with her one step at a time. Does your son get up independently? Does he get dressed and ready for school on his own? Does he have a pleasant breakfast in a timely fashion? Does he get to the bus on time? Do you find yourself still nagging?

She answered yes to all but the last question. Then she said, "But he gets to the bus at the last minute and almost misses it."

I pointed out to her as sensitively as I could that she may have missed the point. Her son had accomplished exactly what it was that she wanted him to accomplish — an independent non-nagging morning preparation. Now it was important for her to see him as successful and to let him know that she was pleased with his responsible behavior. If she continued to see his success as a failure and a power struggle, his behavior would regress to its initial nagging state. Parents who continue to emphasize the power struggle even after it's over, increase the battles. Keep the goal in mind and don't get caught up in the imperfections of the process.

Another example of a covert, less obvious power struggle is one related to a child who feared thunderstorms. This example generalizes to other fears which may have become unconscious power struggles.

Case 2

Andy was afraid of tornadoes. In an attempt to help him deal with his fears, his mom spent a great deal of time explaining the difference between thunderstorms and tornadoes. The more she explained, the more his fear increased. He became hysterically frightened at anything that resembled a tornado. Soon even a brief thundershower paralyzed him with fear. I suggested to his mom that she establish an alliance with her son by saying, "I understand your fear of storms and I know you'll learn to handle it. I'll help you prepare a storm shelter in the basement. You can even have a radio and a blanket down there so you'll be comfortable. When you feel afraid, you may go down to your shelter and stay there where you'll feel safe. The rest of us will stay upstairs unless there's a tornado, in which case we'll also come down and join you."

You can be sure that with that sense of control over his own safety and the disappearance of a power struggle (Mom trying to prove he had nothing to fear), that Andy's overanxiety about storms disappeared. He calmly joined the family during thunderstorms and retreated to the basement only when there really was a tornado warning.

Kent provides another example of diminishing a power struggle.

Case 3

Kent's dad was making a strong effort to build up a good father-son relationship with his young adult son who was home from college. As he approached him to chat, he noticed that he was eating in the living room. That was off-limits for food according to house rules. His dad, annoyed at Kent's disregard for house rules, began by asking him, "Why are you eating in the living room?" Kent found himself in a no-win situation. He could only give an answer that would displease his dad. He knew that there was no excuse that would be acceptable. Instead he walked away without any response. His dad wondered how he could have changed that situation to avoid another power struggle.

I suggested to his dad this alternative conversation. "Hi, son, I wanted to talk with you. Why don't we go into the family room since you're eating? We can talk in there." That would have set the stage for a father-son alliance and not a power struggle. It would nevertheless have also made it clear that the young man was expected to follow family rules. It could have dissipated the power struggle that took place regularly between this father and his son. With practice, father and son became much more effective.

Here's another example for more practice.

Case 4

Ronnie and her teacher were locked in battle. Mr. Rahn had openly criticized and embarrassed her in front of the class. He announced that her work was far below her ability. Ronnie related the story to her mother. Mom could empathically feel the embarrassment her daughter was experiencing and wanted to defend her daughter. Mother's defense would have easily escalated the power struggle between the teacher and Ronnie and would have resulted in Ronnie having an excuse for continuing her poor work. Ronnie might have concluded to her mother, "I can't work for Mr. Rahn. He just doesn't like me." (Does that sound familiar?) Here was my suggestion to Ronnie's mom.

To Ronnie: "I know you feel embarrassed. However, even though I feel badly for you, I think the teacher is right in expecting you to do your work with much better quality. Let's talk to Mr. Rahn together and find out how you can improve your work. Then I'll look it over. I want Mr. Rahn to know what a nice kid and an excellent student you can be."

In a separate communication, the mother might talk to Mr. Rahn and indicate that she was supportive of the teacher's requirements and has supported him to her daughter. She could also share with the teacher the story of her daughter's embarrassment and assure him that she didn't provide her daughter with an "easy way out" of the teacher's expectation. Now the teacher would know that the mother was not encouraging a teacher-student power struggle but was instead dissipating it and supporting a positive relationship.

Mr. Rahn and Ronnie became closer thereafter and even grew to like each other. If the mother subtly supported Ronnie and became too sympathetic to her embarrassment, the power struggle between teacher and student would have escalated.

A further example.

Case 5

Marissa indicated to her mom on the way out the door to the school bus that she was taking with her the family electric mixer because they were baking cookies for a school benefit. Marissa's mother, seeing her expensive mixer leave the house, became visibly upset. Her fiery protest to Marissa was, "You didn't ask me; that's my best mixer; you can't take it and bring it right back here now!" Marissa responded angrily, "I need it today and it's for a good cause. I volunteered it and I have to bring it." Mother's final comment was, "You can't take it; I'm keeping it and you're grounded for taking things without asking. I'll see you after school and talk to you about it then." That power struggle continued after school when Marissa came home angry and disappointed that she couldn't carry through her responsibility to her student committee. The antagonism accelerated during the rest of the week.

Marissa's mom wanted to know if the grounding was an overpunishment, and how she could get her daughter to stop the continuous arguing. She also wanted advice on how to get Marissa to respect other people's possessions.

I suggested to her this alternative strategy. On seeing Marissa about to take the mixer out the door, she could have asked why she was taking the mixer to school. After Marissa's response and in light of the time constraints she could have said, "You can't take that mixer today, but let's talk about it tonight to see how I can help you because I know you're baking cookies for a good cause." That would have immediately relieved Marissa of the pressure of feeling that her mother was opposing her. It also set an appropriate limit since Marissa was not allowed to take the expensive mixer to school.

After school, when Marissa indicated that the project had to be postponed, her mother could say the following:

1. I wish you had asked me about the mixer and given me enough time to think about it, rather than to have just indicated that you were taking it on your way to school.

2. I would have been happy to let you take the portable mixer but this one is too expensive for you to take to school.

3. It's for a good cause and I want to be supportive, so why don't you take the portable mixer tomorrow? Next time be sure to ask me beforehand so that we can avoid the confusion and the embarrassment for you.

4. Absolutely no punishment is necessary. This particular adolescent, a very positive young lady, simply assumed that her mother would support her just cause. She was not considerate enough to ask her mother's permission and was not realistic enough to recognize that an expensive appliance shouldn't be taken to school. Those were both mistakes which she has now learned to correct for the future. Since her mother continued in an alliance with her, instead of punishing or arguing with her, she'll be much more likely to ask for that

permission in the future. If she had been punished instead, she would be determined to get "even" and that would mean continuing the power-struggle relationship.

The commonality of the five "power struggle" examples that I've given provide a framework for suggestions for parents as they deal with children in power struggles:

1. Express enough confidence in your children to see the right things they're doing rather than only the wrong things. If you can redescribe their inappropriate action in a positive way, you'll be setting up an alliance instead of more opposition.

2. In the process of establishing an alliance, be sure not to make another person (other parent or teacher) into the "bad guy." Describe the relationship with the other person in a way that makes that person into your child's ally. This becomes more possible with practice.

3. Do set limits by your behavior and expectation rather than by punishment. Marissa didn't take the expensive mixer. Kent didn't get to eat in the living room. Ronnie didn't get away with poor quality schoolwork. Andy didn't continue to get a lot of attention about his fear of thunderstorms. Brian found that he had the power to get himself to school on time, independently and without his mother's nagging. His mom learned to appreciate that he was accomplishing what she expected.

As you get more comfortable with recognizing that your goal is to teach children to respect limits, and that can be done in an alliance with your children instead of in opposition to them, you'll find yourself feeling less threatened and better able to guide your children positively. You'll see fewer power struggles and so will your children.

2

A United Front

You may have heard your grandparents and great-grandparents talking about parenting with a "united front." That between-parent consistency characteristic of traditional parenting has been superseded in today's society by a priority for open, honest and spontaneous communication. Parents are often advised to share their feelings with their children. They usually don't hesitate to speak openly to them about their own opinions, whether or not these opinions contradict those of their spouse.

In your grandparents' day, the traditional family with two parents was typical. Children in our society frequently have multiple caretakers. Sometimes they are reared in traditional families with two parents. Sometimes they have one, three or four parents. Sometimes grandparents, aunts and uncles take the roles of parents. The statistics on the number of children brought up in single-parent families suggests that it's becoming an increasingly frequent phenomenon. Sociologists, Larry Bumpit and James Sweet of the University of Wisconsin-Madison, projected from their research that half the nation's children will grow up with only their mothers (Jones, 1989).

Regardless of whether children live with one, two, three or four parents or whether their caretakers extend to babysitters, day-care centers, grandparents and

A UNITED FRONT

teachers, it's very key in the parenting of children that those adults who guide their lives do that guiding in a united, consistent way. The term "united front" means that even though the adults may have some differences in their preferred styles of parenting, the view from the children's perspective should be of similar expectations, efforts and limits.

Obviously, with the multiple caretakers in children's lives, it's not possible to have completely consistent expectations, but certainly among those who are the most critical adults, there should be reasonable similarity. If adults are consistent, children will know what's expected of them. They will also understand that they cannot *avoid* doing what feels a little hard or scary or challenging by the protection of another adult.

Parent Rivalry. The subtle competition that exists between parents is hardly ever spelled out in psychology books. Underlying parent rivalry are the parents' concerns about being good parents. Since our society is so competitive, that wish to be a good parent may be operationalized as being the "best" parent. In an effort to prove oneself best, sometimes a parent may cause the other parent to feel that he or she can never be good enough.

While both parents are trying to be best, they may not agree with what "best" means. One parent may see "best" as meaning "kindest." The other parent may view best as being the parent who is respected by their children for setting high standards of discipline. If being the "best" parent doesn't set up contradictions between parents, then they may be able to cope with the competition they feel and come to agreements on values for their children. However, sometimes one parent sees him or herself as best by being kind, caring, loving and understanding. The other parent sees

him or herself as best based on being respected and expecting a child to take responsibilities and show self-discipline. Although each parent sees him or herself in the way that I have just described, they don't necessarily see their spouse in the way that their spouse describes him or herself. The parent who sees him or herself as kind and caring may be viewed by the spouse as being overprotective. The parent who sees him or herself as being disciplined and responsible may be viewed by the spouse as being rigid and too strict. They don't see each other in the same way as they see themselves, so they unconsciously decide that since their own way is best, they must balance out the other parent by becoming more extreme. Therefore, the kind, caring parent becomes more protective in order to shelter the child from the parent who expects too much. The expecting parent believes that he or she must be more demanding and expect more to balance out the overprotective parent. The more one expects, the more the other protects. The more the second protects, the more the first expects. Parents tell me they do this to "balance each other out."

If children are faced by parents who have contradictory expectations, and if these children lack the confidence that they can meet the expectations of one of their parents, they search for the parent who supports "the easy way out." The kind and caring parents, unintentionally, without recognizing the problem they're causing their children, find themselves protecting their children when they face challenge. When children have grown up in an environment where one adult has provided an easy way out for them, they develop the habit of avoiding challenge. They fear taking intellectual and psychological risks since there isn't united parent support for risk taking.

Obviously, the balancing act increases in complexity with three or four parents. Each is desperately anxious to provide the best parenting to keep their children's love. They may compensate for the other parent in either the expecting or protecting direction. After divorce, parents are more likely to believe that they can tempt children to love them by protecting them most, doing too much for them or buying them more.

The rituals that take place in a family where parents have inconsistent expectations are described in the book *Underachievement Syndrome: Causes and Cures* (Rimm, 1986). They are labeled "ogre and dummy games." One, two, three or four of these games can take place singly or in combination for any one child. There are variations of ogre and dummy games which involve stepparents and grandparents and stages of ogre or dummy games which change from childhood to adolescence. The descriptions of these four rituals will be graphic enough so that you can easily imagine how they could happen in your own homes if you don't make specific efforts to maintain a united front. You can also imagine other permutations and combinations of sabotage rituals that could result from alliances between an adult and a child in opposition to the other adult.

Father Is an Ogre. In this traditional family, the father is viewed by outsiders as successful and powerful, the mother as kind and caring. They often appear to be happily married. A closer view of the home life shows a father who has become very negative. He firmly prohibits many of the activities his wife and children wish to pursue. However, the children learn to bypass his authority by appealing to their kind, sweet mother. Mother either manages to convince Dad to change his initial decision, or surreptitiously permits the children to carry out their desired activities anyway. Children quickly learn the necessary manipulative maneuvers. The ritual becomes more extreme because as the children grow older, the father begins to recognize his lack of power over his family. He becomes more authoritarian as he tries to cope with his own sense of powerlessness. In response to his increasing authoritarianism, Mother feels even more obliged to shelter and defend her children. In her desperation she invents new approaches to sabotaging her husband's power in the belief that she's doing the best thing for her children. She literally encourages her husband to become an "ogre" by her determination to protect her children. Although girls in this family may be achievement oriented because they see their mother as powerful, boys will tend to underachieve. They see no effective model in their father, who appears both mean and powerless. They may fear and resent him, but aren't likely to respect or emulate him. They're likely to oppose him and compete with him and choose goals that are counter to his values. Dad may escape to continuous working which further convinces his son to avoid being like his "workaholic" father.

When we look to the history of this marriage, it fits what one usually thinks of as a traditional marriage, with Father serving as the main breadwinner who makes all major decisions. The mother has chosen her husband because she prefers a strong partner. As her husband pursues a meaningful career, she defines her role as "in charge of the children and other household tasks." The final word for parenting the children initially is also Dad's by agreement and by appearances. However, Mother covertly decides that, in fact, she should be the children's protector and guide. She will let him think he's in charge, but in reality, her role as "good mother" will always preempt his power.

The scenario looks like this. The family is sitting around the dining room table eating their dinner. Scotty, a little guy, accidentally pushes over his glass of milk. His dad tells him he's been careless and sends him to his room. Scotty marches up the stairs looking a little sad. Mother thinks to herself, "This isn't fair. Scotty didn't mean to spill the milk. Little children are often careless." As she watches Scotty marching up the stairs she further decides, "This is *my* son. His dad is too strict. He shouldn't have scolded him."

Mother finishes her dinner quickly and unobtrusively ascends the stairway to find Scotty playing quietly in his room. She puts her arm around Scotty and assures him that she realizes it was only an accident. She explains that his father means well but just doesn't quite understand him.

The next day the family sits around the dinner table again. Scotty spills his milk again. This time, since this is a second consecutive spill, Father scolds in a louder voice, warns Scotty to be more careful and insists that he leave the table again. Scotty runs up the staircase screaming at the top of his lungs. By the sound of Scotty's screaming, you would think that his father had physically abused him. Actually, his mother believes that his father has verbally abused him. Most mothers that I interview in our Clinic think that their husbands have louder voices than they do. They don't seem to hear themselves scream. However, they're terribly afraid that their husband's voices will destroy their children's self-concepts. As Scotty dashes off to his room, mother finds she can't continue her meal. She leaves the table, rushes up to Scotty's room, and again assures him that she's very sorry that this has happened. She understands that it was only another accident and apologizes for his father's lack of understanding.

These scenarios may be somewhat exaggerated, however, they illustrate a repeated sabotage ritual which frustrates Father. They empower the son against his father. They cause the son to compete with his dad for his mother's attention and cement a very close mother-son relationship in opposition to Dad. The father feels a sense of powerlessness which he doesn't understand. Father may not even be aware of the mother-son protective tête-à-têtes.

These incidents precede a continuous pattern of mother-son sabotages which Mother thinks of as necessary protections for her child from her husband's wrath. She wishes he wouldn't lose his temper so easily and that he'd be more understanding of his children. But alas, over the years the father-son relationship worsens. Father never does learn to talk to his son and Scotty feels no respect for his dad. Instead there is an awesome fear and a determination to never grow up to be as mean as he. By age sixteen, the act has solidified to a persisting ritual. Here's an adolescent example:

It's homecoming weekend at Smalltown High School and Scotty has arranged for a date and pre-dance dinner. Naturally, he's short some money. He always is. He's not really worried but he does need to go through a three scene drama to get the necessary funds.

Scene 1: Scotty Prepares Mom (Kind Mom)

Scotty: (Confident and assured) Mom, may I borrow $35 for the Saturday night homecoming dinner? I'll pay you back next week.

Mom: Sorry dear, money is Dad's department. You'll have to ask him. I'd like to help you out, but . . .

Scotty: Gee, Mom, you know Dad'll say no.

Mom:　　Well, Scotty, I'm sorry but you'll just have to ask him anyway.

Scene 2: Scotty Asks Dad (The Ogre)

Scotty: (Hesitant, trembling, speaking quickly as if to get it over with) Dad, may I please borrow $35 for homecoming? I promise I'll pay it back by Friday. I'm just a little short because I didn't realize that dinner would be quite that expensive and . . .

Dad:　　(He's behind his newspaper and looks up in disgust) Absolutely not! You get an allowance. You'd better save it next time. Why don't you get a job? You're just lazy. You're never going to amount to anything. (His lecture and put-downs continue. Scotty has heard them all before.)

Scotty: (Retreats silently, head down, relieved to have completed the unpleasant hurdle.)

Scene 3: Scotty Collects (Wonderful Mom)

Scotty: (Head is still down with a tear suitably placed on his cheek.) Mom, Dad just doesn't understand me. (He knows that for sure since Mom has told him that for sixteen years.) Even though I said I'd pay him back, he wouldn't give me any money.

Mom:　　(Withdraws money from apron pocket. This mother always wears an apron. She gives it to Scotty with a kind smile and a hug.) It's all right dear, here's $45. You don't have to pay me back. Have a wonderful time but don't tell Dad. It's from my grocery money. You know, Scotty, your dad really loves you. He just never has understood you.

Scotty: (Hugs Mom briefly) Gee, Mom, you're wonderful! Thanks a lot!

What has this kind, sweet mom done? She has literally made her husband into an ogre — and a powerless one at that. Why would Scotty want to be like Dad? What son would respect a mean father who doesn't truly have the respect of his own wife?

When Scotty was little he said he was more like his mom. As he got older and it became uncomfortable for him to acknowledge similarity to his mother, he preferred to think he was like neither parent. "I don't really know who I'm like," he says. As a matter of fact, he doesn't really know what he wants to do, where he wants to go to school, or what he'd like to major in. He just can't seem to find any direction. But that's all right, Mom'll probably help!

There are variations in the ways that Mom "tried to help" but inadvertently made Father into an ogre. For example, she pointed out to her son that Dad worked much too hard. She doesn't believe any work is worth all the time away from family. The underlying subtle message to son is "don't be like Dad — don't work so hard — life without all that work is more meaningful." The son's application of this concept and his response to his parents by the time he gets to high school, or possibly earlier is, "I don't see why I should do this work at school. It's really only busywork and has no relevance for me. There's much more to life than just schoolwork anyway."

Mom, does it sound familiar? You gave him that message. Unfortunately, he no longer listens, even to you, when you now tell him to study hard and do his homework.

Here's another part of the same ogre sabotage ritual. Dad would like his son to take challenging courses and would like to encourage him in the direction of his own career. Mother protests that their son has the right to choose his own courses, his own career and to "do his own thing." Furthermore, she puts down her husband's career as one that requires too much travel or too much time away from home or too much arguing or does not produce enough salary. The indirect message to their son is, "don't be like your father" and "don't do the things he recommends." The words of the adolescent son emerge as "I want to do my own thing." He knows what he's against: his dad, his dad's career, his dad's course choices and his dad's "establishment." He must choose something that's different and oppositional in order to establish his uniqueness. There's a vacuum — he says he must "experience living." He can't take advice from anyone (except from those who are also doing their own thing — his peers). So he grows long hair, experiments with drugs, or maybe he even joins a religious cult. If he isn't permitted to accept his father as a model, then he must find some other person or group that accepts and notices him and provides a model.

At a time in his life when he could be establishing a positive identity, he invests many years in establishing that identity based only on what he is against. By this time, Mother isn't happy either. Yet she unwittingly stole from her son an ideal role model, the man she loved and chose to marry, her successful husband, the boy's successful father. She made her husband into the man her son must rebel against, "the bad guy," instead of a model he could learn from, and now neither Mom nor Dad understand their son.

Mother Is an Ogre. Sometimes husbands make their wives into ogres. This ritual creates underachieving boys and girls. It includes a kind, sweet husband who would be viewed by women outside of the family as "perfect." He appears generous, loving, warm and even enjoys discussing feelings. He values his parenting role and considers himself a good, fair father. He rarely loses his temper and frequently discusses differences of opinion with his children. They know they can count on him to talk things over and to understand them. Understanding them usually involves seeing things their way. It never occurs to Dad that rivalry exists between him and his wife, although he does see himself as being more fair, more understanding, and the better parent.

Of course there should be some discipline in the home. Children must be guided. Since father is the "good guy," he recommends to his wife that she be in charge of the rules for the children. Mother values self-discipline and clearly sees the need for guidelines for her children. She establishes rules. Now here's the catch: Mom makes the rules — and Dad breaks the rules!

An example:

Scene 1: Rules and Exceptions

The rule is: Children are supposed to do their homework before they watch television. Mother and Father agree to this rule at a family meeting on Sunday. Now it's Monday. Mother walks into the living room to find Todd watching Monday night football.

Mother: Todd, have you done your homework?

Todd: (No response)

Mother: Todd, have you done your homework yet? Todd, remember the new rule we just made.

Todd: Yeah. . .just a minute. Gee, Mom, this is an important play.

Mother: (Leaves the room and returns in a few minutes.) Todd, is the play over yet? You have to do your homework.

Todd: (Looking up briefly) Dad said I could do it after the game — this is really an important game.

Mother: (Leaves room discouraged) Dad said, Dad said — so what can I do?

Scene 2: Father-Son Chat

The game is over. Dad and Todd are sitting on the sofa chatting about the game.

Mother: Todd, you said you'd do your homework right after the game. (To her husband) Dear, remember the rule we made yesterday.

Todd: Gee Mom, Dad and I are talking. We hardly ever have time to talk. I'll do it in a few minutes.

Father: (To Mom) Dear, this should be an exception. Todd will do his work in a few minutes. We were just having a good talk.

Mother: (Leaves room feeling powerless, muttering under her breath) Some rule!

Scene 3: The Shrew

Mother: (Enters, no longer patient and feeling angry, speaking in a loud tense screeching voice.) Todd, you better do your homework. You'll fail your course. It's ten o'clock. You can't talk all night . . .

Todd: Gee, Mom, why are you yelling? You could just tell me. I'll get it done. It's too late to concentrate now. I thought I'd go to sleep and get up early and do it in the morning.

Father: It's okay, dear, no reason to lose your temper. Todd will do it in the morning. He'll get it done and it will go much faster after a good night's sleep. (To Todd in a patient voice) Good night, son. Have a good night's rest. Be sure to do your work in the morning.

Todd goes off to bed thinking that his mother is really a nag and resolving to do his work in the morning. Father settles down in front of the TV wondering how his wife became such a shrew. Mother sits down with him in front of the TV feeling drained, angry at herself for losing her temper, wishing she could get her husband to help her and sensing that somehow she's powerless. She knows for sure that Todd won't do his homework. When the alarm goes off in the morning, he'll go back to sleep. Even after the snooze alarm goes off twice and she calls to him three or four times, he'll barely be able to pull himself out of bed; and when he whizzes down to "just miss the bus," Dad will offer him a ride to school on his way to work. She feels exasperated. She knows she'll attend the next

parent-teacher conference without her husband and again hear the teacher say, "Todd is such a bright boy. If he could only use his brains to do his work instead of figuring out ways to avoid it, he'd be an excellent student." Todd becomes a bright underachieving mystery to his teacher, to his mother and, much later, to his dad as well.

The "Mother Is an Ogre" ritual fosters Underachievement Syndrome in boys and girls. Girls underachieve in this family because they see their mother as powerless and an ogre, certainly not an appropriate role model. They'd prefer to be "Daddy's little girls" and effortlessly please and manipulate Daddy. The boys in this family are happy to identify with their father. They like being "powerful and kind." Unfortunately the message they receive from Dad doesn't encourage achievement. It's a passive-aggressive message to ignore Mother, to ignore teachers and to ignore rules. It's a message to "do your own thing," to avoid demands of others and to procrastinate until you feel ready. The readiness rarely comes.

Daddy Is a Dummy. This ritual is a slight modification of the ogre play and is found mainly in homes where mothers are psychologists, educators or have taken a recent parenting class. Their husbands, on the other hand, may be doctors, engineers or truck drivers but haven't taken the parenting courses. The main difference, of course, is that the mother has learned the "right" way to bring up the children and the father hasn't. Therefore, Mother decides that it's her responsibility to give Father directions on how to rear Bobby correctly.

Mother knows for sure that boys require daddies as appropriate male role models, so she explains this to her husband. He's delighted. He has visions of going off on fishing trips and watching football games with his son. Initially, he's told he must play with his little boy to get the good positive relationship started. So he coos and goos to him; he feeds him and he even changes his diapers on occasion. Sons are fun! So far things seem to be working out well. Father is delighted and pleased that his wife knows all about child psychology.

Somewhere around age two the problem begins. Dad is in charge for the day and he finds Bobby exploring and destroying his books and papers. His work is in a shambles. Father loses his cool. He picks up his little boy and spanks his bottom half a dozen times and puts him in his crib screaming and crying. Mother enters to find the living room strewn with papers, Father distraught and her angelic son screaming desperately in his crib. She begins Step 1 of her first-aid psychology by immediately taking Bobby out of his crib, comforting his hurts and explaining that everything will be all right and that Daddy just lost his temper. "Poor Daddy."

Bobby is calmed down so she moves to Step 2, which is to explain to Father (in front of Son) a better way to handle this kind of dilemma in the future. She indicates that he must explain to his son the appropriate behavior and refrain at all times from scolding or spanking. Positive reinforcement is effective but punishment is harmful to his self-concept and will cause his son to resent him. Father listens patiently as he applies his own first aid to his strewn and crumpled papers that cover the floor. He wonders why he lost his temper and he feels terrible about possibly damaging his son. He's most willing to try again and he resolves to use only positive reinforcement. After all, his wife took the parenting courses and she should know.

Dad tries again. And he tries again. Each time he seems to lose control. Each time he ends up "damaging his son's self-concept." "Maybe," he thinks, "women are just better at bringing up children. If he could only put off playing with his son until the boy is a manageable size, he could probably do better. Perhaps he'll go back to school and get another degree, or he could certainly devote more hours to his work at night. If he worked on Saturdays that surely would improve his opportunities for promotion and he could earn more money and, in the long run, he probably could do more for his son."

Dad's conclusion: I'll work hard now and play with Bobby when he's older.

Mom's conclusion: I wish Bob wouldn't have to work so much, but he doesn't handle the children very well anyway, so at least I can get them on the right track.

Bobby's conclusion: Daddy's never home. All Daddy does is work. That's dumb. I sure don't want to be like Daddy.

At about this time, the "daddy is a dummy" tune reverts to the "father is an ogre" melody and the song is played out as it was in the first orchestration.

Mother Is the Mouse of the House. The dummy ritual for mothers, which results in rebellious adolescent daughters, begins in a conspirational relationship between Father and Debbie. It's a special alliance which pairs Father and his perfect little girl with each other but, by definition, gives Mom the role of "not too bright" or somehow "out of it." During early childhood, Daddy never says "no" to Debbie. She has a special way of winding him around her little finger. Mother

admires the relationship, but from early on she doesn't quite understand it nor is she really part of it. Father and Debbie go off hand in hand, looking with wonder at each other. Debbie knows Daddy is easier on her and admits that she can do things when her dad's at home that she would never be allowed to do if Mom was also at home.

Preadolescence arrives and Mother notices a subtle, and sometimes not-so-subtle, battle taking place between Debbie and herself. She's not exactly sure why, but Debbie can't seem to take the slightest criticism from her. As a matter of fact, if Mother says "black" Debbie says "white," and vice versa. As Mother loses her temper in frustration, the voice of "Father, the great mediator" emerges from the other room. "Now girls, would you stop your arguing. Let me see if I can help you settle things." Or even worse, Dad says to his wife, "Dear, would you please stop screaming at our daughter. I don't see why you two can't get along. I don't have a problem with our daughter at all." He, of course, directs this criticism to his wife within his daughter's hearing. The arguments continue and increase in quality and quantity. Dad mediates, smoothes things over and helps Debbie to feel better, always at Mom's expense. Mom just doesn't understand why it is that she feels so out of control with Debbie nor does she understand why it is that they always argue. When asked what they argue about, Mom says, "I don't know, just anything." When Debbie is asked what they argue about, she responds, "We just argue."

Then Debbie enters junior high school. Father begins to worry about his perfect little girl. He remembers when he was a teenage boy. Dangers lurk in the corridors, in the lavatories, at school dances and at parties. Father initiates a tirade of cautions about

90

cigarettes, alcohol, drugs and, of course, teenage boys. He must protect his perfect daughter from the evils of growing up, but Debbie says, "Dad, don't you trust me?" Dad answers that he trusts her but he isn't so sure about the rest of the world and so he decides it's time for rules.

Rules mean "*nos*" and Debbie has never really received a no from her father and *no*s feel terrible. She appeals to Mom. She reminds Mom that she was once a teenage girl. Mom is delighted at this new relationship with Debbie. She believes that they stopped arguing because Debbie is maturing. Now she colludes with Debbie and offers to be a support to her. Debbie explains her dilemma and Mom assures her that she'll talk to her father about permission to stay at the party later than he ruled. Mom talks to Dad and convinces him to relent and Debbie has discovered a new manipulation. Now she manipulates with Mother against Father. When that works, she continues to manipulate. When Mom's alliance doesn't work, she returns to try Dad. First she manipulates Mom against Dad, then she manipulates Dad against Mom.

The double manipulations continue for several years and Debbie is in senior high school. Suddenly, Mom and Dad are aware that Debbie has been manipulating both of them. They decide that it's time for a united front. It's time for consistency. It's time to be on the same team.

Now Debbie asks for permission to stay at a party until 12:30. Her father says, "No, 12:00." She begs Dad. "Please, Dad, pretty please with sugar on it." Dad persists. Debbie retreats to Mom. "Mom, you were a teenage girl once, remember? Can't I stay a little later? All the girls are staying out later."

Mom says no. Dad says no. Now Dad and Mom are on the same team. Debbie stands alone against them.

They're saying no and even when she does her best manipulating she can't change their decision. She feels desperate. She proclaims, "My parents are controlling me. They used to treat me like an adult and now they treat me like a child." She goes to the party and stays out until 2:30. Her parents are anxious, scared, and worried. When she walks in the door they can smell the alcohol on her breath. They ground her. First they ground her for a weekend. She says she doesn't care. Then they ground her for a week. She says that doesn't matter. Then they ground her for three weeks. She says, "You can't ground me." Finally, they ground her for life! When she's grounded for life, she can do most anything and she does. They have completely lost the opportunity to guide Debbie. She is immersed in opposition and she finds antiparent friends to support her.

Now Mom and Dad are really anxious. Debbie is in with the wrong crowd. They've found cigarettes in her room. How can they trust her? Mom tries to talk to her, but that never worked. Dad tries to communicate his concerns. That's a little better but not really effective because he wants her to stop smoking. She won't. She says she has to be her own person and that her parents must stop being so controlling. She says they don't respect her. Her parents read her journal that she leaves out on her desk. They know from the journal that Debbie "hates" her parents, her father only a little less than her mother. She's disrespectful, uses foul language, ignores their rules and her formerly *A* and *B* grades have dropped to *D*s and *F*s. She skips classes and argues with her parents and her most frequent words are, "stop controlling me." They no longer can control Debbie and they can't understand what happened to that sweet, perfect, little girl. She has joined a group of "druggies" or "burn-outs" or "dirt balls" (varieties of antiparent,

antischool rebels) and she just can't wait until she can get out of her parents' controlling home.

The parents bring Debbie to my office. She doesn't want to come. She plops herself down in the chair across from me, determined that I won't help her and says in a disdainful tone, "My mother is stupid. You'd think she was born 100 years ago."

"And your father?" I ask, wishing I didn't have to hear the answer.

"He's not much better — well maybe a little better. Neither of them know how to live. I really can't stand them. I can't wait until I get out on my own. I'm counting the days."

The rebellious daughter, who had too much power as a small child and whose father unwittingly encouraged her to compete with her mother (who should have been his first love), feels rejected, unloved and out of control. These girls take various paths but they all signal the same sense of lack of power, which they feel mainly because they were given too much power as children. Some girls express their feelings of rejection by parents in a pattern of promiscuous sexual relationships. They say their parents (especially their fathers) don't love them anymore and they must have love. When they're in a boy's arms they mistakenly believe that he loves them and it feels good. When they leave that bed for the next one, they feel rejected and embittered and easily accept the next invitation that looks like love.

Other girls express silent rebellions; bulimia, anorexia nervosa, depression and suicide attempts are powerful ways of expressing feelings of loss of control. These illnesses leave parents feeling helpless and blaming each other. They put the adolescents or young adults in control of their parents but not in control of themselves. Fathers who conspire with their little girls to put Mother down as the "mouse of the house" can expect to suffer through adolescence.

How to Avoid Ogre and Dummy Games. The key to avoiding Ogre and Dummy games is **respect.** If parents voice and show respect for each other, children will respect their parents. Ogre and Dummy games can be corrected by parents simply by their recognition or awareness of their existence. Parents don't usually require therapy to make these changes.

Here are some suggestions:

1. Make it clear to your children that you value and respect the intelligence of your spouse. Don't "put that spouse down" except in jest and only where it's absolutely clear that you're joking. Use conversations with your children to point out the excellent qualities of your husband or wife.

2. Be sure to describe your spouse's career in respectful terms so that you or your spouse aren't feeling as if you're doing work that the other doesn't value.

3. Don't join in an alliance with your child against your spouse in any way that suggests disrespect. Sometimes parents do that subtly, as in, "I agree with you, but I'm not sure I can convince your mom (or dad)." If you communicate to your child that you value his or her other parent, it will almost always be good for your child, for your spouse and for you. Be particularly careful during adolescence. Just a few slips may initiate rebellion.

4. Reassure your oppositional children frequently of their parents' mutual support for them. However, be positively firm in not permitting them to manipulate either of you. They'll be quick to see spouse support

of each other as a betrayal of themselves and will feel hurt and depressed. Since they're in a habit of seeing relationships between others as betrayals of commitments to them, you should assure them frequently that spouses can respect each other while both still love their children. This is a difficult reality for these youths to cope with, and they may feel emotionally isolated unless they're reassured. One of the parents (the "good" one) will be placed in the position of mediator by these children, in order to persuade the other, unless the parent absolutely refuses to play that role.

5. When your children come to you to complain about their father or mother expecting too much of them, they do that because they're hoping that you'll support their easy-way-out position and that you'll side with them. They're hoping you'll help them "get out of" what the other parent has asked them to do. You want to respond in kindness while maintaining a message of respect for your spouse. If the child says, "Mother or Father expects too much of me," or "Mom or Dad is always yelling at me," examples of appropriate answers follow:

> "Your mother expects that of you because she knows you're capable. If she didn't expect that of you it would mean that she didn't believe you could do it. You should be pleased that your mom expects it. It really means she values you. Mom expects it because you can do it. After you do it, Mom will be proud and you'll feel good."

Here's another example of an appropriate response I recently heard in our Clinic:

The father had asked his son, Josh, to pick up the living room. Josh hadn't done it and his father scolded him and reminded him that he ought to pick up right away. In the process, Father lost his temper. Sixteen-year-old Josh came to his mom, rolled his eyes disrespectfully and complained, "Dad's yelling at me again."

When Mom and Josh used to play ogre games, Mom recalled that she would have protected her son. This time, after one appointment at our Clinic, she knew better and she said, "Dad wouldn't have had to yell at you if you had picked it up the first time." The boy showed an expression of shock for a moment, but immediately turned to pick up the room. In this new response, Mother clearly supported Dad and Josh knew what he was expected to do and did it.

These kinds of responses, whether related to Father or Mother, give children a message of confidence. Most of all, they provide the united fronts that permit your children to build self-confidence through achievement.

Why Do We Sabotage?

A mother and father sat before me in our Clinic looking puzzled and said, "I guess we sabotaged each other. No wonder we're powerless with that kid. It's like 'shooting yourself in the foot'!"

Why do we do it? Why do we sabotage our spouse? Is it competition with our partner? Do we want to be the better parent? Probably that's accurate, partially.

What about that wonderful sense of intimacy that we feel when we're baring our soul to someone, to our very closest genetic relation, our own child? Are we so desperate for closeness that we prioritize that intimacy before the closeness of our marriage relationship?

We all know that adolescents establish closeness by talking negatively about other kids, that unions build solidarity by confirming that administrators are bad guys and that nations build patriotism in the face of enemies.

Whether our alliances with our children against our spouses are attempts to deal with our personal loneliness, to establish our expertise as parents, to feel good about ourselves as being sensitive to our children's needs or to build solidarity with our children, or all of the above, these alliances surely cause problems for our children. They also adversely affect our marriages and our children's future marriages. In these insecure times of prevalent divorce, are we perpetrating infidelity to our spouse in the name of good parenting? These are some hard and heavy questions to think about the next time you confide in your child about your spouse's problem parenting.

Abraham Lincoln addressed our nation as he faced the hard decisions that led to the Civil War and concluded, "A house divided against itself cannot stand" (1858). Perhaps this important observation about our country has even more applicability within our families.

When Parents Love Their Children But Not Each Other

The ogre and dummy games that take place in a family during or after divorce, or in a newly blended family where there are stepparents, become much more complex and are somewhat more difficult to cope with. Although many children in our society go through divorce, it continues to be traumatic almost regardless of their age. It can't be assumed that divorce is more traumatic than living in an unhappy marriage. That comparison would be difficult to prove. If you, as parents, are going through a divorce, there are ways in which you can help your children to adjust to the divorce situation and lessen the trauma they feel.

The key to children's post-divorce adjustment is the adjustment of the mother and father to the after-divorce relationship. The children are faced with feeling love for both parents despite the fact that their parents don't love each other. The parents, in turn, may both love the children and may be afraid that they'll lose their children's love. Children often feel caught in the middle and may worry that if they express love to one parent, the other parent will no longer love them and vice versa.

As parents help their children cope with divorce, they should give children assurance that they'll be loved and that they may continue to love the other parent. They should receive positive descriptions *of* both parents *from* both parents. Sometimes that may feel difficult in the anger of divorce. Here's a case example:

> A mother of a teenage girl and a preadolescent boy went through a traumatic divorce when her husband had an affair with another woman. The father decided that he was in love with that woman and wanted the divorce. The mother, who had earlier thought she had an excellent marriage, felt rejected and angry. During the several separations that preceded the divorce, she tried to explain to her children, most particularly her daughter, about their father's "childish and immature behavior" in an effort to deal with the situation which she could not explain rationally. The daughter agreed with her mother that her father was behaving childishly.
>
> Later in counseling, the daughter shared with me activities that she was involved in with her dad; going to concerts and wearing

inappropriate tee shirts of which her mother didn't approve. Her mother had blamed her dad for offering these experiences to their daughter. Her daughter acknowledged that she had asked her dad for these experiences although she knew her mother wouldn't approve, but hadn't told her mother that she had asked. Before the divorce even became final, the teenage daughter had begun manipulating her mother and her father. Although the dad wasn't intending to hurt his daughter, in his efforts to keep her love he was giving her a "sabotage" message that said she could ignore her mother's limits. Not only was this girl feeling caught in the middle between her parents but she was learning to manipulate each of them in ways that would eventually make her feel insecure and angry. If the pattern had been allowed to continue she would have become a rebellious and depressed teenager.

Children tend to manipulate their parents after divorce, often unintentionally. Parents are vulnerable because they are competing for their children's love and are afraid to lose their children to the other parent.

After divorce, emphasize positive achieving aspects of the other parent so that he or she can be a constructive role model. Children will see that person as a role model even if you describe the parent negatively. The more emphasis you put on the negative characteristics of the other parent, the more likely it is that your child will feel helpless to do anything about his/her own negative characteristics which are similar. If it's difficult to find positive characteristics about the other parent, don't say anything at all.

Children who live with and visit parents in separate homes should have two locations where they receive love, where they learn to work and make effort and

THE EASY OGRE

where they can play and have fun. That kind of arrangement provides a real sense of consistency and security for them despite divorce. Of course, that requires good communication between parents and that's not usually easy. One home which is all work in contrast to "fun and games visitation" has the effect of making the work parent into the ogre and encouraging children to think of the visitation parent as "the easy way out." Here's an interesting case variation:

James, a ninth grader and the older of two boys lived with his mom who had been divorced for approximately three years. He was positive, responsible and an achiever in school. When I asked him about his visitation to his father he said that when he visited his dad it was a lot like a hotel. He had few responsibilities. He didn't have to pick up or clean. They went out to eat. I then asked him if he enjoyed that easy lifestyle assuming that he did. He responded, to my surprise, by saying no. He really rather enjoyed being at home with his mom. He described the difference between homes as, "My father is liquid, my mother is solid." He felt better about the responsible kind of life-style that he was handling at home than he did about the "fun and games" visitation.

It's important to mention that although neither mother nor father were remarried, mother had several family friends in the neighborhood who provided good male role models for James and permitted him to join with their families for activities.

It's equally important to know that Mike, his younger brother, was underachieving and loved his dad's "hotel way of life." Mike is doing

104

well now, but it did require some changes and some new friends as "role models." Dad became disinterested in the boys soon after our therapy began.

Especially after a divorce, continue to treat your child as a child. Too many times the oldest child becomes the parent's confidant and is given adult status. The result is that although the child enjoys the power of being an equal adult, at a later date, if the parent tries to set limits or tells the child he or she cannot do something, the child won't accept child status. The child may become rebellious with the very parent who had originally awarded him or her the adult status. Power given is not easily taken away.

Although both parents should assure their children of their love (if both continue to be available), it's unnecessary and even harmful to assure a child that you'll always love him or her more than anyone else. Parents do give that message frequently to their child. It is likely to result in the child feeling unloved and rejected when the parent chooses to remarry. The child isn't willing to share the parent's love with another adult or with future siblings. He or she has learned to be comfortable only with first place. A child who has been given the power of a spouse is likely to exhibit anger and aggression when they feel displaced by a parent's new adult friend.

Don't feel guilty about the divorce. No one is perfect. Guilt has never helped improve parenting skills. You're human and doing as well as you can under the circumstances. Time will heal the feelings of hurt and will put problems into perspective for your children. Do get some counseling to help you through the trauma of your divorce and do get brief counseling for your children. They'll want a safe person to talk to and it will prevent them from feeling caught in the middle, particularly if both parents agree to the counseling.

A summary of suggestions for single parents, whether resulting from a divorce or other circumstances, from my earlier book (Rimm, 1986) is included in Inset 2.3.

INSET 2.3 - SUGGESTIONS FOR SINGLE PARENTS

As a single parent are you destined to have a problem underachieving child? Of course not, but your job is more difficult. Here are some simple rules to guide you — simple only in that they're few and straightforward. In reality, they're terribly difficult for single parents to negotiate. Pat yourself on the back for each successful day. You deserve it. Now the rules:

1. Find a career direction for your life to give you a sense of purpose and to build your self-confidence. Making your children your only purpose gives them power and pressure that will be too stressful for them to manage.

2. Find some adult social outlets for yourself. Don't feel guilty about enjoying yourself as an adult.

3. Find a reliable babysitter or day-care center facility for your children. Consistency in care givers and surroundings is very important for children.

4. Treat your child as a child — not a toy to be played with nor an adult to be depended on. *Do not* share your bed with your child (except during thunderstorms).

5. Take time (I know you have little) to enjoy your children's achievements and encourage them to take responsibilities.

Now two special rules for single mothers parenting boys.

1. Boys should have an older male to serve them as a model. Find effective role models for your boys — uncles, grandfathers, teachers, Boy Scout leaders may all be helpful to your son in learning to be comfortable with his masculinity.

2. If you don't view your children's natural father as an effective role model, absolutely don't tell your boys how much they look like and remind you of him. Also, avoid power struggles with him. If their father mistreats you and shows open disrepect for you, your sons are likely to imitate this powerful but disrespectful behavior.

These rules will sound simplistic to some and impossible to others. They may be difficult for a single parent to live by, but they are effective for parenting your children. Review them regularly.

Some final words about divorce and single parenting — they're not easy for children or for their parents. If there is even a five percent chance that your marriage may improve by counseling, make the attempt. All marriages go through crises and many marriages improve with outside help and problem solving. Many parents have assured me that they have appreciated this advice which helped them keep their marriage together. Don't give up on your marriage if there's any hope of improving it. Children benefit when the marriage stays together effectively and most children suffer through divorce.

Abuse - When There Can't Be a United Front

There are some home situations where a parent is put in the position of not being able to support their children's other parent. Circumstances which involve verbal or physical abuse or alcoholism require protection for children. You should not whitewash or ignore that abuse. You must take an advocacy and sheltering role for your children. Your children, who are living in an environment where there can't be a united front, are going to suffer from the effects of an alliance with an adult against another adult. However, that's much less harmful than the suffering that comes from physical or verbal abuse by a parent. Your first step in dealing with an abusive situation is to provide protection for your children. Second, make it clear to the abuser that your children will be protected. Their safety comes first. Once you've found shelter, you'll want to explain to your children why you've taken this protective position.

When there has been physical abuse of either a parent or of children, be careful not to build the abuser into a meaner and more powerful person than he or she really is. Continuous talk about the abuse won't

COUNSELING CAN HELP

help the children nor the situation. It's best after you've explained the abuse situation and listened to the children's concerns about the abuse, that you go on from there. Be willing to listen if they wish to talk, but don't assume you should rediscuss, reexplain, reexcuse or recondemn the abuser. Continuous talk may encourage more feelings of anxiety and powerlessness. You and the children may require some professional counseling.

An important problem for parents is diagnosing the difference between real abuse, borderline abuse and nonabuse. When a parent physically or sexually abuses a child, it seems obvious that one ought to be able to identify that as abuse. However, parents do have the right to spank children. That may not be the best form of punishment, but it certainly is within parental rights. One parent could consider the spanking appropriate punishment for the children's misbehavior while the other parent may consider it physical abuse.

Identification of abuse can become complicated. For example, Father spanks. Mother tells him he has no right to spank and tells him this within the children's hearing. Children act even worse because they know that Mother is defending their position against Dad. That makes children more powerful and determined to act out. It causes the father to feel more frustrated and powerless and, therefore, to spank more. In that kind of situation, you can see that abuse wasn't intended and shouldn't be so interpreted. If the mother feels that spanking is inappropriate, she should defer her judgment about the spanking because it doesn't qualify as abuse. She should discuss the difference that she has with her husband. If she protects or defends her children against their dad's spanking, she perpetrates further problems.

Here's another example of a questionable abuse situation. The child does something careless without thinking it through. The parent calls the child an idiot. We all know that parents shouldn't call children idiots. Yet probably thousands of parents have called them that or such similar "put-down" names in occasional anger or frustration.

How do you deal with that kind of situation? If one parent considers it verbal abuse to call the child an idiot and the other one considers it just a way of describing a child's dumb behavior, the best way to resolve the difference is humor. If that doesn't work and if the child comes to the parent and says, "Mom shouldn't have called me an idiot," Dad should simply say, "You really acted pretty dumb. Your mother doesn't really think you're a idiot. Next time think about what you're doing. I guess we all act like idiots sometimes." In that way, you let the child know he or she need not take the label of stupidity seriously. On the other hand, you also remind the child that you expect him/her to think. Your statement doesn't show disrespect for the other parent.

Calling a child an idiot or dumb or stupid once in awhile won't destroy him or her. Children are resilient enough to handle a few "put downs." I wouldn't categorize the occasional inappropriate name-calling as abuse. However, a parent who continuously uses terms which make children feel stupid or dumb may cause them major confidence problems in the future. It's something that parents should *definitely not* continue to do.

These examples describe situations where one parent might describe an activity as abuse while the other parent might describe the behavior as a temporary poor parenting technique. There will be borderline situations that become even more difficult

to define. For these, it's better not to take the child's position but to talk the problem through with the offending parent. It will be less harmful to the child. Maintain the united front if parent discussion can assure you of improvement in the future. In real abuse, don't enable the abuser. Protect your children.

The Parent-Teacher United Front

Read this section with the assumption that most teachers became teachers because they want to teach children. They usually care about and wish to make a positive difference for them. Now you may say that you could prove that this isn't the case with some of the teachers who have taught your children. A small percentage of teachers may feel and act "burned out," may not want to teach anymore, never really wanted to teach or thought teaching would be something different than what they're experiencing. Despite your occasional negative experiences, I would nevertheless maintain that most teachers care about teaching children well.

Parent-teacher conflicts emerge mainly because some teachers have different philosophies about teaching children than some parents. Some parents believe that their philosophies are better than those held by their children's teachers. The parents may be right. It is possible that their approach might be better for their children. The teachers may also be right. It's equally possible that their approach would work more effectively. So the issue really is that when teachers and parents disagree on how children should be taught, we have a mismatch in philosophies which could destroy the united parent-teacher front.

Now if educational philosophies between teachers and parents differ in directions that encourage children to do more than the teacher expects, they probably won't cause children any problems. They'll continue to receive a message of responsibility. However, if the philosophy of the parents differs from the teacher in providing an "easy way out" for children or if it describes the teacher's philosophy as inappropriate, irrelevant or boring, it provides an excuse for children not to accomplish what the teacher expects. Although the parents may make appropriate points about their analysis of the teacher's philosophy, the parents should not be sharing their positions with their children if there is the risk of permitting them to subtly escape from school responsibility.

Consider that your children are sitting in the classroom and are faced with tasks or assignments, some of which are interesting, some not so interesting, some tiresome and some repetitive. If they've received the message from you that these aren't worthwhile projects, why would your children consider it important to fulfill the teacher's expectations? They know that they can come home and find an empathic ear in their mother or father who basically agree that the assignment was inappropriate to their interest or intelligence, their use of time or for some other reason. If you want your children to achieve in school, give clear communications of respect to your children about teachers in general. Let them know that teachers are people who are devoted to children and to making a difference for our society through education. If you give them that message about respect for educators, it will go a long way toward encouraging them to feel positive about their teachers and about school. It will be likely to make a great difference in their entire attitude about school learning and achievement.

Children should hear how much you value their teachers. Now that's no small issue since, in my experience, there have been parents who have globally done just the opposite. If you suggest to children that teachers are "not too bright" or only "go into teaching because they're not capable of doing anything else," or "don't deserve the salaries that taxpayers pay them," those references which serve to put down teachers might as well be messages to children to not perform well in school. They aren't expected to respect their teachers and won't.

Sometimes teachers who are also parents give negative messages about their fellow professionals. Their children are listening. Subtle statements which make it appear that you don't respect teachers cause problems. Here are some examples:

Todd, a fifth grader, considered himself to be a debater. His parents proclaimed that, indeed, he would make a fine lawyer. He exercised his arguing skill specifically with teachers and not only provoked arguments but persevered beyond reason and respect. In his arguments he attempted to put his teachers down. At home, Todd had a good relationship with both his parents except that he argued continuously with his mother in that same haughty "tone of voice."

In counseling, it became clear that his father had inferred that teachers were "not very bright." His mother was an active leader in PTA. Her activities were referred to by his dad as "busywork." His father, in essentially describing the teachers' and his mother's activity as unintelligent, was inferring that Todd was more intelligent than his teachers and his mom. This encouraged Todd to try to prove that neither teachers nor his mother were as smart as he. Thus, the continuous arguing and the resulting underachievement.

Here's an example of a positive communication with a teacher:

Susan, a third-grader, complained to her mother and dad repeatedly that her teacher didn't like her. The parents were anxious about their daughter who was less and less willing to go to school. She complained about illnesses and made excuses for avoiding school. The parents handled the difficult situation with responsible communication. At conference time they explained to the teacher what they were hearing from their child. They indicated to the teacher that they were assuming that the teacher didn't dislike their daughter, but only wanted to let her know what their child was saying.

Within one week, Susan's attitude changed. Her teacher gave Susan only a little extra, temporary, positive attention which seemed to be sufficient to make her feel approved of again. The avoidance and anxiety disappeared and the problem was solved in a respectful, positive way. The parents never agreed with the child about the teacher's supposed dislike. They never even shared with the child their conversation with the teacher. They simply conducted the adult communication in an adult, respectful way and the problem disappeared.

Selecting Your Children's Teachers

If you, as parents, were able to select your children's teachers, it would be more likely that you and those teachers would be united in an educational philosophy for your children. It doesn't necessarily mean that you would select the teachers that teach your child best, but it does mean that you and the teacher would be more likely to agree. For example, sometimes parents

who are oversolicitous and cause their child's dependency, select a teacher that is also oversolicitous and encourages their child's dependency. That may be a totally wrong teacher for that child. Nevertheless, there would be much less opposition between you and that teacher. Since opposition between parent and teacher might cause more harm than oversolicitousness, your child would probably continue to benefit by the choice.

If your child has had a negative past school year, you should informally investigate whether you, as parents, can recommend or select a teacher for your child. Schools vary a great deal in their policies about honoring parent requests for teachers. Some have formal policies while others have informal guidelines. You aren't likely to be able to specifically select a teacher, but many schools will permit you to suggest the teacher that you would like for your child. The principal may assure you that he/she will make the effort to facilitate the chosen classroom arrangement. Principals can't guarantee that they will follow through on your choice, because if many parents select the same teacher, it would obviously cause the principal major problems.

In some schools, the child's present teacher may make a recommendation for the following year. In that case, you may want to discuss with the teacher your preference for the following year. Again, the teacher won't be able to provide a guarantee, but it may be worthwhile for you to initiate the discussion.

Most schools don't advertise their policy of permitting parents to request teachers. There's a good reason for that. If they announce the parent privilege, then parents might feel obligated to select a teacher for their children. The principal might feel pressured to honor their requests. This could cause an impossible situation for the school. You should subtly investigate the informal or formal policies in your school. If you're privileged to make requests, don't advertise it to the parents of your children's friends or they, too, may ask for the very same teacher. That will result in too many requests to be honored. When you ask for a teacher, don't in any way put down the other teachers. Recognize the principal's overall responsibility for placement of all children in the best-matched classrooms.

Exceptions to the Parent-Teacher United Front

There are those times where regardless of how hard you try, you feel like you just can't support a united front between you and your child's teacher. There may be curriculum issues that you disagree with, general philosophies of education, a sense that your child and a teacher are in a particular power struggle or an attitude about discipline that you feel is inappropriate for your child. Your first priority is to show sufficient respect and humility to communicate to that teacher about your concern. Don't accuse the teacher of being wrong. Ask the teacher questions about what you're hearing from your child rather than assuming that your child is communicating accurate information. Don't report the problem to the principal unless your initial efforts with the teacher don't work and there is potential harm for children in the class.

Curriculum Differences. In cases of intellectually gifted children, there may be dramatic differences in philosophies among teachers. There are some who believe that gifted children should do all of the assigned work whether or not that work is a challenging or appropriate learning experience. In gifted education, we call that busywork. Children who already know or could learn the information with much briefer assignments, may turn off to what they view as irrelevant work. As parents, with a good understanding of your child's capabilities, you may find yourselves siding with your child against the teacher's inappropriate adjustment of curriculum. I'd recommend that you take the responsibility for communicating to the teacher the child's concerns, without assuming that the teacher is wrong. I would also suggest that if there's a gifted coordinator or gifted consultant in the district, that you suggest a potential meeting between the teacher and the consultant to talk about your child's special abilities.

Although you may have taken all those steps appropriately, some teachers don't believe in educating gifted children differently. There's a real possibility that even these appropriate adult communications won't affect change in your children's curriculum. Your next step will be to indicate to your children that although you realize that they could learn better or faster, that they should complete the teacher's requirements well. Suggest that they do them quickly and efficiently and use the extra time to do independent learning projects at school or at home with you. Let them know that you're interested in sharing learning with them. In that communication, you won't provide children with an easy way out. You do provide them with the information that you recognize that not all teachers agree on the way that gifted children learn. You haven't indicated that you don't respect their teachers. You've shifted the responsibility for learning to your children by expecting them to take further initiative in their education even when it's not provided appropriately by their school situation.

You, as parents, should take a proactive stance in the school district to provide gifted children with appropriate curriculum. Plan to be positive, patient and

120

persevering. Meanwhile, for your children, there is no easy way out. They may be spending some time on "busywork" which they consider boring, but they will be learning the reasonable conformity and the jumping of required educational hurdles that may be necessary as they continue through high school and college.

There are some requirements in our schools which simply are not appropriate for all children. Nevertheless, they'll probably not do any harm. A little extra practice or drill, despite the fact that children may know the information, may even be helpful. Even if it's true that they're experiencing boredom when it might be better for them to have a more exciting learning experience, they will survive the "trauma." Most children are resilient enough to cope with the challenge of boredom.

Physical or Verbal Abuse. Sometimes a more extreme exception to a united parent-teacher front is required. If parents believe that a teacher is being abusive to children, whether it's physical or verbal abuse, they have the responsibility for providing protection for their children. Classroom abuse is wrong and children deserve to have a safe classroom.

The first step again is to take the courage to meet with the teacher without accusing the teacher of abuse. Indicate what's been reported by children in the classroom and tell the teacher of your concern. Give the teacher a chance to either change or defend the behavior. If the reports continue, the second necessary step is to communicate to the principal or to the teacher's immediate supervisor. Even in severe cases, it will be important not to unintentionally give your children permission to misbehave or challenge that teacher. As a matter of fact, your message to your children should be that there's little danger of their being abused by their teacher if they behave appropriately in the classroom and pay attention to their work. In no way do you give your child permission to be disrespectful to a teacher.

If the abuse is genuine, you must be a strong advocate for safe classrooms. Do join forces with other parents who voice similar concerns. Be an advocate for children, but remember, be positive, patient and persevering and don't center your life and that of your children on discussing the issue constantly.

Sexual Abuse. Children are often too frightened to report sexual abuse by teachers. They may only hint to you that a teacher is making them "feel funny" or that a teacher gets uncomfortably close to them. The suggestion of strange behavior deserves your immediate follow-up discussion and clarification. Do explain to your child their right not to stay in a student relationship that feels uncomfortable and encourage them to report any further suspicions to you immediately. Don't overreact but **do** bypass the teacher and communicate your concerns to the principal.

If your children have been physically or sexually abused by a teacher, you will want to handle this difficult situation very carefully. Your children may be asked to testify in court. You and they may feel justifiably indignant about how the school administration or the courts are treating the abuse. Although you and your children will be coping with a difficult emotional problem, don't make the mistake of permitting the problem to monopolize your lives. As the abuse and the children become the center of attention, you will find yourself in an alliance with them against the court or the school. Despite the good cause, the children can be empowered too far by the battle advocacy. As they hear parents talking continuously to neighbors, teachers and each other about the abuse issue, your children may begin to focus all their attention on the incident. Assure your children that you will support them in their testimony and that you will persevere in your attempt to provide safe classrooms. Help them to understand that they are not required to feel responsibility for the problem. Let them know that you, their parents, will be their advocates, but that they should go on with their own activities.

Here's a case example that illustrates the high risk of getting children overly involved.

> Katy had reported that she wanted to drop fifth-grade band. When her mother asked her for her reason, she responded that her band teacher made her "feel funny" in band class by coming too close to her. Based on that description, the mother permitted her to drop out of the band program. Her mother asked her if there were any other concerns that she had, but she voiced none.

> A year later, it was discovered that the band teacher had been sexually abusing several girls in the class by touching them inappropriately. It was difficult to determine if the abuse was real, but after testimony of several students in the class, it was determined that there was abuse. Katy and her parents became advocates for the teacher's dismissal. Police hearings and court testimony followed and the decision was made to change the teacher's school and require therapy for the teacher. He was not dismissed from the school district.

> Katy and her parents were indignant. It was the topic of constant home discussion, as were the many plans for attendance at school board

meetings and protests. Although I supported Katy's parents' concern relative to advocating for school safety, I believed that the issue was becoming overwhelming for their daughter. I pointed out that Katy was now centering her entire attention on the issue and was thereby deriving a great deal of power and attention. She was at high-risk for depression, under-achievement and oppositional behavior in school after the court case was over, regard-less of the result. Fortunately, my advice to the parents came in sufficient time so that they could gradually ease out Katy's involve-ment. Katy's immediate response to her noninclusion, even though she was assured the problem would be taken care of, was a temporary depression. The parents were prepared and were able to help Katy move beyond the abuse case. Otherwise, Katy, with her parents, would have become involved in-tensively in an adult, oppositional struggle which may have caused her more adjustment problems than the uneasy feelings that she felt around her band teacher.

The Teacher-Parent United Front

Although most of this section has been directed to you, as parents, it's equally important that teachers give a message of support for you. If teachers aren't sup-portive of parents and aren't saying positive things to children about them, they may render parents power-less to follow through on teachers' suggestions or recommendations at home. Teachers should be especially careful not to talk to other teachers negative-ly about parents. That may easily happen when parents volunteer in schools. If children hear about the opposi-tion between teachers and their parents, it may have

an adverse effect on the parent-child-school relationship. A message of respect for parents, given by teachers, facilitates children's learning in school and at home.

A Grandparent, Aunt, Uncle-Parent United Front

Occasionally, I'll see children whose underachievement or school learning has been more adversely affected by differences between grandparents and parents, or aunts and uncles and parents, than by differences between parents themselves or between parents and teachers. Particularly when children are brought up in households where there are other adults serving as caretakers, differences can be dramatic and traumatic. Sometimes the power struggles that used to take place between Grandmother and Mother affect how the grandmother treats her grandchild. It almost seems as if Grandmother is trying "to get even." In effect, it may provide an easy way out for a grandchild if Grandmother and Grandchild form an alliance against Mother.

Inset 2.4 includes some recommendations for grandparenting.

Aunts and uncles, particularly those who don't have their own children, sometimes provide an easy way out for parents' expectations of their nieces and nephews. In some ways, they may be continuing former sibling rivalry patterns through children. Aunts and uncles can have a delightful relationship with their nieces and nephews provided they give messages of respect for school and parents.

If you have sisters or brothers who are sabotaging your parenting power, be firm with them. Let them know how you feel and about your expectations for your children. If they continue to sabotage your

126

INSET 2.4 — DOs AND DON'Ts OF GRANDPARENTING

DOs

Do love your grandchild as much as you would like.

Do keep communication strong by regular telephone calls, letters and pictures.

Do give special gifts that might be hard for parents to afford to buy. Be sure you have parent permission.

Do share stories of your own childhood and encourage children to tape your stories. They give children an appreciation of their past.

Do play competitive games with them. Don't just let them win. They should learn to win and lose.

Do make things or have projects together. Sometimes parents don't have the time. You have skills that children will enjoy learning.

Do read to them and listen to them.

Do support their parents and say only positive things to children about their parents.

Do tell them how important school and education are.

DON'Ts

Don't spoil them by giving them too many toys, gifts and money. They will become "gimme" kids who have too much and don't appreciate what they have or what you have given them.

Don't encourage them to do things of which their parents don't approve. That will be like sabotaging their parents' power.

Don't do things for them that they can do for themselves. It's important to encourage their independence.

Don't permit them to manipulate you against their parents. That will hurt them, their parents and you in the long run.

Don't put their parents down or indicate that you disagree with their parents. Be supportive. They and their parents need your support.

parenting power, ask them not to visit. They're doing harm to the children whom they love. For the most part, however, once they're aware of the importance of a family united front for children, they'll be willing to disregard the competitive feelings that they may have with you and, instead, recognize what valuable and loving relatives they can be to your children. Many children have very close, caring relationships with aunts and uncles.

The Sibling United Front

As you learn to cope with your parent rivalry, it will make it easier to understand sibling rivalry. Sisters and brothers may also love each other and continue to feel that their "smartness," beauty, athletic prowess, musical success, good behavior, etc. are valued only compared to the absence of such successes for their siblings. In our competitive society, it is difficult to prevent competition from invading the family relationship. Yet ideally, we would wish that family relationships could provide a cooperative shelter from competition.

A parent united front will help to minimize sibling competition since children will be less likely to take sides with one parent against the other. However, sibling rivalry is not likely to ever be eliminated, nor should it be. If there are no brother/sister struggles in your family, you may assume that one child is giving orders and the other accepting those orders. Children should have differences and should be assertive enough to express and even argue these differences. Thus, some sibling quarrels and fighting are a healthy indication that none of the children are completely submissive. Part of your children's experience involves learning to problem solve when there are differences.

An important guideline for parents who are coping with sibling rivalry is not to try to mediate or 'ferret out' which child is to blame. Parents should first attempt to ignore their children's arguments so that the children may work them out themselves. Often it is more effective for parents to time themselves out (preferably in Bermuda*) rather than timing-out their children. The attention you give to the rivalry usually serves to reward the fighting behavior. That is, each child tries to get the parents on his or her side. Your mediations are likely to increase the extent of the rivalry.

Not debating children's arguments and not taking sides are the first steps in handling family sibling competition. Do set a limit for a reasonable noise level or aggressive behavior. Reserve the option of separating the children for fifteen minutes or half an hour. Any two different rooms will do. They don't necessarily require an official time-out. Of course, they will probably soon want to be back together again.

In addition to withdrawing attention from the arguments, try to build positive and cooperative relationships. A token reward system can be used temporarily to reinforce children for their cooperative behavior. That works well particularly when parents are finding that their siblings are required to spend a great amount of time together, for example, during summer vacation or a long car ride. By dividing the day into two or three sections, children can receive a point for each time period of cooperative behavior. Early morning to noon might be one section of the day. Afternoon to dinner or evening meal would be a second section, and the evening meal to bedtime would be a third

*This suggestion is courtesy of Michael Cornale, the assistant director of Family Achievement Clinic.

section. Siblings would only receive a point if both children are being nice to each other. That encourages their cooperation. The goal is to accumulate a small number (10 to 15 points) toward an activity in which both children can participate in, like going out for pizza, going to a movie or renting a special video. You'll know that your program has been effective when one child hits or teases and the other one says that it doesn't bother them because he or she knew it was all in fun. That's a real confirmation of the children's cooperation. Accept that as being an earned point. No token reinforcement system works for long, but this will be effective at particularly stressful times.

Another approach to building cooperative sibling behavior, is using surprise planning. When one parent gets the children together to plan a surprise for the other parent or for a third child, then the children get involved in cooperative planning and feel closer. An alliance with a positive goal builds unity. The secrets of gift giving, surprises and parties seem to unite brothers and sisters and diminish arguing. Planning something special for Grandma, Grandpa, Aunt, Uncle, a neighbor or a friend encourages a sense of togetherness that comes from joint efforts. Parents can effectively use cooperative strategies multiple times to build a sense of sibling solidarity within their family.

Sibling rivalry almost always affects children's achievement. Children tend to easily assume that their achievement appears more impressive if their brothers and sisters performance is not as good. Explain to your children that it's nice to have a "whole smart family" and that achievement by one child doesn't limit achievement by the others. We suggest that children be encouraged to admit any feelings of jealousy. Most children have them. We teach them to handle these feelings better by accepting the challenge of openly admiring their sisters or brothers. That seems to help everyone and minimizes the "put-downs." We tell older siblings that younger children usually "down deep" think their older siblings are wonderful. They want to be just like them.

If your children put each other down, don't take sides at the time. However, you should communicate your concern to the one who is doing the "putting down" in privacy. There's a much better chance of improved behavior if you don't correct the child in front of siblings.

As parents of achieving or underachieving children, your attention should be directed at effort and positive performances so you don't find yourself reinforcing, by your attention, your children's lack of achievement. Don't appoint your achiever to the role of tutor for your underachiever. It will serve only as a "daily put-down" for the other. He or she may not understand or be able to express those feelings. Children often say they appreciate the help but it makes them feel dumb.

Mainly, be patient and avoid taking sides. The two children in our family who did the most arguing, Eric and Sara, are delightfully close as young adults. I wish I had known that as they were growing up.

3

Habits that Facilitate Achievement

It takes about two weeks for persons to form new habits. That probably means that children will take at least that same amount of time to break old habits. There are a few important habits and routines that we teach children at the Clinic that encourage independent achievement behavior. These will increase their educational effectiveness and efficiency and decrease your nagging. Responsible habits facilitate children's success in school, thus increasing the likelihood that they may become lifetime learners.

Homework and Study

Schools vary in their expectations of homework and study and children vary even more in their response to school expectations. Achieving children study mainly at a desk or table in a quiet place although some listen to music. Underachievers (children who do not achieve to their ability level), however, exhibit a great many troublesome study habits. Many believe that they study best lying on their bed, headset on, watching television while reading something over once, quickly. They would consider intense study to be reading the material over twice in that same position. Other underachievers do homework only after they're nagged, scolded, reminded and supervised. Even then, they protest and avoid quality work. A third group of children sit with a parent nightly, certain that they can't complete their assignments without that parent's assistance and direct supervision. Finally, there are some underachievers who simply don't do homework or study at all.

As parents of children who may be in one of the last four groups, you may wonder how your children fell into such bad habits and why other children have better habits.

The next section will assist you in helping your children change to better study approaches. If your own children already have good study habits, read on nevertheless. There are also some suggestions for good studiers.

A Time and A Place. Good study habits begin with an appropriate time and place for study. A good time for study will have to fit with individual children's other activities as well as their parents' schedule. However, some general rules can guide you in setting both time and place.

Children's demonstrated history of responsibility for schoolwork should determine if parents should set their time for study. If children are accustomed to accomplishing homework independently and have a record of getting homework and study completed well, there's no need for parents to specify a time requirement for study. On the other hand, if children haven't been studying enough, they should have their time structured. The amount of time should vary with their grade and school requirements. Elementary school children should study from one half hour to one hour; middle school, one hour to one and one half hours; high school, one and one half hours to two hours per evening. In some highly academic high schools, three or more hours may be required.

Immediately after school there should be a break for children to have a snack and some physical activity. They often believe that they should use that break to watch television. However, television puts children into a passive mode and they're unlikely to want to leave television to begin study. Thus, for you to move your child from television to study will probably involve a massive power struggle. It's better to insist that television follow study and homework. It's likely that your children will say, "But I need to relax after school." Please assure them that they will get to relax. Exercise is both relaxing and energizing. It's more appropriate after a day of sitting. Certainly time to chat or talk or clown around or play are also appropriate for after school — but not television.

In determining time for study, not only should there be an opportunity for an active break after school, but there should be something to look forward to after study. If possible, at least part of the study time should take place prior to the evening meal, leaving time after study for play or television. If the study time is set late in the evening, study is not likely to be as efficient. Children often tire after dinner and there would not be time after study for play. When study time is late, children often sit at their desk preoccupied with daydreaming or half dozing. With only bedtime to follow, they aren't motivated toward efficiency. For some reason, unbeknownst to adults, very few children seem to enjoy going to sleep. They often manipulate ways to stay up to get adult attention. Homework or study may become a "stay up late" manipulation if study time is placed prior to bedtime. If children say they have completed all of their homework and have only filled a fraction of their allotted study time, they may use the remainder of the scheduled time for reading over material, organizing notes or doing extra reading for future book reports or for pleasure. Always reassure them that as their achievement habits improve, you will be more flexible and allow them to set their own study schedule.

A study place is equally important to providing an atmosphere where children learn efficiently. Classical conditioning research provides the psychological rationale for having an appropriate place for children to study. I often describe Pavlov's research on conditioning dogs to children in our Clinic to persuade them to study at a desk or table in a quiet atmosphere. The story that I tell and suggest that you share with your own children, points out how conditioning affects unconscious involuntary behaviors. Why you should study at a desk in a quiet place is included in Inset 3.1.

INSET 3.1 — HOW TO TELL YOUR CHILDREN HOW TIME AND PLACE WILL IMPROVE THEIR STUDY - THE RESEARCH

A physiologist by the name of Ivan Pavlov was doing research with dogs to determine how much they salivated when eating. While the experiment was taking place, Pavlov's assistant observed a serious problem. The dogs began salivating when the caretakers entered the room *before* they received their food. Pavlov's assistant believed that the research was therefore spoiled. Pavlov, a very creative scientist, recognized what we call in science, a serendipitous finding. He discovered some very important principles which are now known as the laws of classical conditioning.

When two stimuli are paired together over time, the second begins to cause the same response as the first. In other words, since the caretaker always brought the food, the dogs associated the caretaker with the food and, therefore, began salivating at the sight of the caretaker (even before they had the food).

In the same way, when you sit in the same position for studying daily, your automatic responses will be conditioned to concentrate when you assume your study position. This will make it easier for you to automatically concentrate and make good use of your study time.

Children who prefer studying in the dining room while visiting with siblings or who prefer noise, often explain that they can't concentrate or study at a desk. After I've explained classical conditioning, I indicate to them that they have been classically conditioned to relax when they are socializing with family members or watching television. It will thus be easier to relax, but more difficult for them to concentrate on study-ing. When children assert that they study better while lying on their bed, I ask them what they associate with lying on their bed. Hopefully, their response is sleep or rest. I again point out that the conditioning for sleep doesn't encourage their active involvement in their study. They're conditioned to rest, fall asleep and not concentrate when lying on their bed. I ask them to con-dition themselves to sit in a position where they can become actively involved with the material, have good light, are more likely to take notes and concentrate on the material, until that becomes a habit. I point out to them that adults who were good students in college often went to a study carrel in the library or a quiet place in a room where everyone was studying and where there wasn't any social life.

Sometimes, it's difficult to convince children to ac-cept an appropriate time and place but Pavlov's story usually gets them started. You should be firm and in-sist for two consistent weeks. Once study place and time become a habit, you'll find you're no longer nag-ging them. They'll automatically go to their desk in their room to do their homework and that will enhance their concentration and their efficiency.

How Parents Can Help (But Not Too Much). There's another advantage in separating your children from their parents and siblings for study. Children who are too dependent and who are likely to ask questions before they've tried to solve problems on their own are less likely to ask those questions if their parents are physically located at a distance. Since we're encouraging independence in learning, it becomes important for your children to take the initiative to work out their homework on their own before they ask for unnecessary help. Don't sit with your child nightly doing homework. It's their responsibility to do their own homework and your responsibility to take an interest or monitor where appropriate. You may answer questions only after your children have made a determined effort to work on the material on their own. You may also work with children on special projects. However, even on these special projects it becomes important for you to be the "guide on the side" rather than to get so heavily involved that when the project is done, it's not very clear to your children whether you or they completed the project.

If your children have already begun independent habits, then you won't have to remind them about study and should only share with them those materials which they ask to share with you. Show interest, but don't impose. For example, reading a story they've written or checking for errors in a first or second draft of a composition might be an appropriate assist if they request it. Discussing ideas with your children is also suitable. Quizzing spelling or Spanish after study is fine as a show of support for their study. Teaching them a strategy for study is certainly a help. Sharing an interest is always appropriate.

For children who have had a history of underachievement or dependence, you'll be required to take a more active role (see Inset 3.2). First you'll want to help your children set up strategies for independent work. You'll want to monitor their work on a regular basis to be certain that they're completing quality homework.

INSET 3.2 — ENCOURAGING INDEPENDENT HOMEWORK

Dad: Troy, I've talked to your teacher and he assures me that you have very good ability. Now that I know that, I want you to get in the habit of doing your schoolwork on your own.

Troy: Gee, Dad, I just need Mom's help. Can't she just help me a little bit? (A few tears) I just can't do it without her.

Dad: No, neither Mom nor I can help you because we really want you to prove to yourself that you can do it, but we have some good ideas that will make it fun.

Troy: (Sad face, but listening)

Dad: We'll start by moving Grandpop's old desk up to your room so you can have your own study space.

Troy: (Faint smile of interest)

Dad: Then we'll set up a study time. Your teacher suggested that one hour a day for a sixth grader would be about right. So we'll start with that. Of course, that's only for five days. You get two days free of homework. If your work seems to be very good and you don't need that much, we can cut that time down. Of course, if you don't finish your work in an hour, you'll have to work longer than that. That study time will be in your room, at your new desk, before watching any TV and with no radio or stereo on.

Troy: Dad, that definitely won't work. I have to watch cartoons when I get home to relax and unwind after school.

Dad: Son, that cartoon watching will have to wait. I like to watch TV to relax too, but when I sit down to TV, it's really hard to get up to do any work. So I wait to watch TV until after I've finished my work. You'll have to do the same thing. I don't mind if you have a snack or sit around or go outside for 15 minutes, but by 4:15 I expect you in your room working and absolutely no TV until you're done and I've checked your work. That way you'll be all done with your study time before dinner and we can shoot some baskets after dinner and watch TV when it gets dark.

Troy: I know this just won't work. My cartoons aren't on at night. I think I should watch TV for half an hour before homework.

Dad: Troy, part of this new homework plan is that you're going to earn some fun things for doing your homework on your own. It's not that we're really paying you for homework, but we thought it might help you to make a game out of it. Now you'll want to think of something you could save up for.

Troy: (Full smile) Gee, Dad, that sounds neat. What kinds of things can I save for and how do I get the prizes?
(Rimm, 1986)

Be careful not to do too much. Ask your children to review material at least three times before they ask for help. If they don't understand the instructions or material you may explain one example. Then permit them to complete a second example to be sure they understand. You may suggest strategies for completing the work or you may help break it into manageable steps if they feel overwhelmed. You could even recommend a study or learning approach. After that, be sure your children go back to their desks in their rooms to complete the assignments. When they've finished their work, they should bring it to you to review. Do an overall review of their work. If it's carelessly done, simply insist they go back and complete it well. If they've misunderstood and done it incorrectly, then patiently go over one or two more examples. Next, send them back to complete it correctly. If, for the most part, they've done good quality work and it looks mainly correct, don't take away the teacher's responsibility. There's no reason to correct every example. The paper should be brought into class for teacher correction. Your message to your children should be that they've done good work and it's time to take a break for some fun.

You may wonder which parent should help your children. Often mothers are assigned to schoolwork supervision. Either mothers or fathers can help children. However, in the case of boys, it's helpful if Father takes the major responsibility for helping or monitoring schoolwork, particularly if the child has not been performing well in school. That doesn't mean that Mother can't help for some subjects or times. If Mom is the only person who monitors schoolwork for her son, and if Dad is available, it becomes very important for Dad to communicate clearly to his son about how important he believes schoolwork to be. He should tell his son that he'll be checking with Mom regularly to be sure he's doing his work. Boys seem to have problems if only their mothers take responsibility for supervising schoolwork. They assume that it's not masculine to be concerned about education. As they mature, they see education as less relevant since their dad hasn't shown an active interest.

If you're beginning a new study routine with your children, a contract may be helpful. Some guidelines for contracts are included in Inset 3.3 and some sample contracts are included in Inset 3.4 and 3.5 and in the case study about Peter.

INSET 3.3 — CONTRACT RECOMMENDATIONS

Rita, a sixth grader, had become a habitual homework forgetter. She rarely studied and never studied independently. She always insisted on her mother's help. I pointed out the importance of developing her independence and her prompt handing in of assignments. She had heard that before. I also explained that I knew she had some bad habits that would not be easy for her to change.

We set up some positive and negative consequences that would help her to change those habits. She was delighted with the reward system we offered her but angry about possible punishments. After some reassurance about the temporary nature of our game plan and my explanation of why she would never be punished as long as she handed in her work, we agreed to the following contract.

Rita, her mother and father and Dr. Rimm agree that Rita will do homework and study at her desk in her room for at least one hour a night, five nights a week. She will show one of her parents her completed work daily. If her teacher reports there are no missing assignments on Friday, she will earn 10 points. When she has accumulated 100 points, she may choose a friend to go with her to the theme park for a day. If there are missing assignments, she will not be allowed to go to the Friday night basketball game with her friends unless she can show her parents that she has completed all assignments by game time.

Rita
Mom
Dad
Dr. Rimm

Rita did miss two basketball games. She earned her day at Great America Amusement Park in twelve weeks. At that point, a new contract was negotiated. The times that Rita did not have completed assignments, she tried to argue with her parents to convince them of the importance of the basketball games and that almost all assignments were completed. Her parents didn't argue. They simply reminded her of their agreement. She went stomping off to her room, slamming the door behind her, but she didn't go to the game. That first time was harder for her parents than for her, but the clear limits were effective. Notice that no extensive punishment was required and that the parents did not increase the punishment despite the stomping.

146

INSET 3.4 — SAMPLE STUDY CONTRACT

Troy, his mom, dad and Mrs. Norbert agree that Troy will spend at least one hour each day, five days a week, studying and doing his homework independently at his desk in his room. He will do this before he watches TV. There will be no radio, stereo or TV on in his room during study time. After his work is complete, his dad will review his material and together award him points which Troy will save up toward the purchase of a bicycle. Troy's mom and dad will not remind him to study and he will take the initiative independently. This agreement may be changed only by mutual agreement of the undersigned.

Troy
Mom
Dad
Mrs. Norbert

(Rimm, 1986)

INSET 3.5 SAMPLE STUDY CONTRACT

David, his mom and dad and Dr. Rimm have agreed to the following organizational and quality improvement plans:

1. Organizational Plan
   a. Folders which are labeled for subjects
   b. One side unfinished work, the other side completed papers
   c. Folders reviewed once a week and cleaned up
   d. Hanging organizer for locker
   e. Braided bracelet for reminders for after-school responsibilities
   f. Bring *all* folders home every night
2. Quality Improvement Plan
   a. $1 for each weekly *A*
   b. $3 for each grade point average of *B* or better
   c. $1 for each tenth of a point grade improvement/weekly above personal weekly best

---

Motivating Them to Study More

I've provided you, as parents, with the rationale to provide to your children for why they should study efficiently. Nevertheless, you will find that many children will not wish to change their bad habits. They'll continue to provide you with all kinds of reasons why their old way works better. I'd suggest that you ask them to experiment in one or more subjects. They may select a priority subject to which to make their commitment. Convince them to add fifteen minutes a day to their study time. If they add fifteen efficient minutes to what they normally would have done, it will be sufficient to increase their grade by at least one level. They can expect to go from F to D, D to C, C to B, or B to A. If they're willing to make the extra fifteen-minute time commitment using techniques described in this section or a study technique taught by their teacher, they will find that they can be effective in raising that grade. Remember, we're trying to teach them the relationship between their own personal effort and the grade outcome. They really don't believe that study techniques apply to them nor do they think that study will improve their grade. Convincing them to try one subject may be sufficient for tempting them to adapt more effective study processes. This approach works very well in our Clinic for increasing children's motivation for improved quality of work once they've learned to get all their assignments in on time. Some children are more resistant than others. The case of Alice is an example and will give you insight to the underlying fear.

Alice, a sophomore, was completing all her homework and was putting some time into study for tests. Her B and C grades now matched her high average ability. However, in

148

Spanish, Alice's test grades were *D*s and *F*s. It was not difficult to convince Alice to put more time into study, but it seemed impossible to persuade her to study effectively. Even for her final exam, she avoided using the techniques I had recommended. She was completely honest in admitting that she ignored my advice. Finally, I asked, "Alice, is it possible that you don't want to improve your Spanish grade?"

Alice's answer unveiled her underlying fear of not being smart enough. She responded, hesitantly, but insightfully, "Suppose I do study the right way and I still get a *D*?"

How-To Study Hints

I have suggested to you that, as parents, you can give children some direction and strategies for study. Following are some hints that may be helpful to you as you guide your children. Remember that their study must be effective for them to develop that sense of ownership for their efforts. If they have inefficient or poor study habits or don't know how to study, then of course, they're likely to assume that study doesn't make a difference. I've already shared with you the importance of setting a time and place for your children to make a commitment to real study and you now know that it will be difficult to convince them to take the risk of real study. Now, for some techniques. There are many books written on study habits that are more complete than this chapter, but I've included some tips that seem to make study differences for children who come to our Clinic.

Using All the Senses. We know that children show variations in the ways they learn best. Some children learn more efficiently visually. Others are more effective

149

listeners and prefer auditory learning, and still others learn best by tactile senses or through hands-on activities. Stories which involve feelings or emotions enhance learning for most children. Using all four styles can encourage your children to utilize their strengths in the learning process. For visual learners, writing, copying and drawing or collecting pictures will reinforce their memory for information. For auditory learners, listening to tapes, talking on tapes and oral repetition will assist in improving their memory. Kinesthetic children will learn better by manipulating counters, markers or flash cards. Teaching children to make up stories, rhymes or mnemonic devices will assist all of them in involving their feelings or emotions in improving their memory. Teach your children to discover what works best for them. Using as many senses as possible for studying will help.

Often when I've spoken to teachers, I've shared stories of my fourth-grade teacher, Miss Shoobridge, a white-haired lady who was very close to retirement. She was my favorite teacher. I recall that she spoke in a quiet voice so that we had to listen very carefully to hear her. She always shared wonderful pictures from her own travel as well as beautiful nature pictures from the Audubon Society. We also learned to use maps and globes. I loved to touch the continents when it was my turn to go to the map. What I remember most in my fourth-grade class were the stories Miss Shoobridge shared with us. She was so "human" and not just a teacher. She had a real life outside the classroom. I hadn't imagined that teachers did. She had feelings and touched my emotions.

How can it be that after exposure to so many teachers, in so many grades and in so many subjects, I can recall so clearly what Miss Shoobridge taught me?

Perhaps it was her use of all the senses that strengthened my recall. Her stories and pictures of her travels and experiences reinforced my memory of explorers, continents, national parks, birds and animals. I remember her description of Ponce de Leon and his search for the Fountain of Youth, even to the extent that I recall the question that I asked her as well as her answer. The question I asked was, "Why would any man want to look for a fountain of youth?" (It seemed so silly to me then.) Her response to me was, "Some day you'll understand, Sylvia." Yes, Miss Shoobridge, I do understand.

As you teach your children to remember information, encourage them to use all their senses and their emotions. You may become as effective as Miss Shoobridge was for me. After all, parents are teachers, too.

Memorization. Appropriate use of memory is extremely important for children's successful performance on tests, yet children know little about how to memorize material. Some children seem to automatically learn and other children have intuitively sorted out memory techniques. There are some psychological concepts which will help all children to understand and use their memory better. I explain to our Clinic children about short-term and long-term memory. Try the explanation which I use (Inset 3.6).

Inset 3.6 provides the rationale I give to children for explaining the importance of their active involvement in the study process. The more actively they're involved, the more likely that the information will be moved into long-term memory storage. There are some specific subject study hints which will generalize to improved memory. These are included in the next sections which I've addressed directly to your children. As parents, you may read these to them or copy the pages to share with your children.

INSET 3.6 — MEMORY

Short-term memory is a temporary storage area for information. For example, if I gave you a telephone number and you immediately made a telephone call using the number, then had a conversation with someone, after you'd hung up the telephone, you would no longer remember the number. It's as if the number had gone "in one ear and out the other." It didn't make any permanent traces or lines on your brain and the number is literally gone from your memory.

If information isn't moved from short-term memory to long-term memory, it can't be retrieved unless it's very meaningful or you have an extraordinary memory. Thus, when you read something over once or twice, unless the material is especially interesting to you, you can't remember it for use on your test.

All of us recall times when we sat with a book in front of us and read the material. Then after we put the book down, we had no recall of what we'd read. The feeling you have when you take the test after that kind of perusal of material is best expressed by, "What's wrong with my memory? Why do other kids do better?"

Long-term memory provides much more permanent storage. The information that you move into long-term memory makes traces or lines on your brain and those traces can be retrieved and recalled for testing. In order to move material from short-term memory to long-term memory, you have to 1) make it meaningful, 2) organize it, and 3) rehearse or practice it. All those strategies will cause that information, boring or otherwise, to move to long-term memory for retrieval for your test.

If you study the same amount of time but study the right way so that the information is moved to long-term memory, you'll have the nice sense of confidence that comes when you feel smart when taking your test. If you study the wrong way, you're likely to feel "dumb" because you think your poor performance is due to your poor memory. Would you rather feel smart or dumb?

154

Note Taking. When you take notes from a class lecture, whether it be social studies, science or English, leave a very wide margin at the side of the paper. At night during study time, review your notes and write summary statements or key vocabulary words in those wide margins. Before your test, cover the key words or sentences and recall the notes you made in lecture or cover the written notes and recall the key words in preparation for your test. Talk aloud to yourself or write these explanations as you study. You may wish to talk and write.

Study From Textbooks. These are some suggestions for studying social studies, science, literature or other subjects where you must read for verbal information.

1. After reading each paragraph, write down a summary sentence of the paragraph in your notebook. That summary sentence can be used for later study.

2. At test time, make up a test question for each summary sentence. Your questions should be the same type that your teacher usually uses, whether multiple choice, matching, true-false or essay. This will be excellent active preparation for your tests.

3. If your teacher tends to expect you to recall definitions on your tests, then write key words and their definitions as you study initially. When you review for your test, quiz yourself using those key words. Don't just study them orally, since the tests aren't given orally. Instead, study in the same way the test is given. Write the key words and write their definitions. Then check back to see whether your definitions are correct.

4. If you've made up test questions that are essay questions, select a few of the most important essay questions to answer. Write out the essays for the best practice. Although your teacher's questions may be different, they will probably incorporate much of the same information.

Learning Math Facts. If you're in first, second or third grade, you're often required to study addition, subtraction, multiplication and division tables. For some children this is a simple task. However, even for some very bright children, this task is a challenge. It may be that anxiety or tension interferes with your memory. It may be that you find the memorization boring. The best way to study these facts is in written form and to review the same tests many times so that you have rehearsed the process in writing. Time yourself on the same test over and over again, always trying to beat your own time. The more you time yourself at home, the less tense you'll feel in school and finally you'll be master of those basic facts.

Studying for Math Tests. Save all your past homework to prepare for your math tests. Then redo from scratch at least one homework problem from each assignment and match your new answers to those that were already corrected on your homework. The hardest problem from each assignment will usually be sufficient to review for an exam. If you just read or look over examples you will probably be poorly prepared for your math test. If you don't get **actively** involved, you haven't studied sufficiently.

Spelling. When you study spelling, you should do that in writing rather than orally, unless you're practicing for an oral spelling bee. If spelling bees are given in your classroom, you should study both orally and in writing. The old-fashioned method of folding a paper vertically into four columns remains appropriate for the study of spelling. Copying the word first from your book, then covering it up and writing it in the next column, checking back, covering it up, writing it in the third column, then checking back again, covering up all three columns, and writing it the fourth time and checking back, will make you into a super speller. Your parent's quizzing you for spelling is inappropriate for written spelling tests. Oral quizzing won't hurt you and may be done if you and your parents enjoy it, but only after you've completed your written spelling study.

Foreign Languages. Teachers often ask students to prepare flash cards to study foreign language vocabulary. While flash cards are helpful, the teacher's testing approach should be the prime determinant of how you study. For the most part, children are asked to either write vocabulary words or write definitions. Therefore, flash cards are a good mechanism for collecting the vocabulary for study. Instead of practicing flash cards orally, you should use those flash cards to write either the appropriate vocabulary words or the appropriate definitions. That's especially important to improve foreign language spelling. Many students lose points on tests because they've spelled words incorrectly or left off accent marks. That happens mainly because they've studied verbally and haven't studied in the way that reinforces or helps them memorize correct spelling.

Finding Ideas. Children and parents feel frustrated when children are asked to write a composition or do a social studies or science project and find it difficult to get started. Children often procrastinate, wait until the last minute and sometimes even avoid doing their assignments because they feel so overwhelmed. A story

157

that is often told to me by children who don't get assignments in or do assignments at the last minute is that they have spent lots of time thinking of how to get started, but haven't been able to come up with a good idea. Sometimes they even ask their parents for topics. Parents frequently respond with suggestions that they feel are appropriate. However, the children trap those parents into power struggles in which the parents give topics and the children respond by saying the ideas aren't any good. They may go back and forth and finally accept one of their parent's suggestions but aren't willing to carry that suggestion through because first, the suggestion was their parents', not theirs, and second, they really don't like the suggestion. So although parents are really trying to be helpful they find themselves feeling helpless.

Children who are seeking good ideas, criticize themselves continuously. They can't find ideas that feel good enough and thus they avoid getting started. Sometimes children tell me that this happens especially in their strongest subject. If they think they're good creative writers, for example, or very good in social studies or science, they particularly feel afraid to complete a project. They're afraid it won't be as good as they should be doing, considering that this is their known area of expertise. They're feeling pressure. An example of a plan for getting ideas for special projects is included in Inset 3.7. Other systems your procrastinators may find useful are included in Inset 3.8.

Children who are taught techniques for idea production begin to incorporate these approaches into their general thinking and develop the confidence that dissipates passivity and perfectionism. Encourage these techniques by teaching them and by personally modeling them. Incorporate them into your own problem-solving approaches.

INSET 3.7 — IDEA FINDING PLAN FOR A SCIENCE PROJECT

1. Gather up science books from around the house and your school science books. Take these up to your room at your desk.

2. Get pencils and pad.

3. Leaf through books and daydream a bit about ideas you see.

4. Write down any possible project ideas.
   a. They can be silly.
   b. They can be hard.
   c. They can be impossible.
   d. They can seem dumb.

5. Don't criticize any of your ideas; just keep writing.

6. You can put some ideas together.

7. You can borrow ideas from books or pictures or other kids.

8. Remember, don't criticize any ideas.

9. If you run out of ideas from books, look around the room; you may see some more. Look out the window to find even more ideas. Anything can be on your list.

10. Try to write down at least 30 ideas before you stop.

11. Now go back and look over your list.

12. Cross out the ones that don't interest you or seem truly impossible.

13. Leave four or five in your list that look pretty good.

14. You may wish to combine a few ideas.

15. Think through your plans for those four or five.

16. Bring your plans for those and have a little meeting with Mom and Dad. They can hear all about your plans and can help you if you should want a little bit of help. I know you'll be able to find ideas this way because I've tried it and it really works.

17. Set a time schedule for the completion of your projects. Be sure to include more time than you need.

18. Make a list of the parts of your assignment and check each accomplishment as you finish it.

(Rimm, 1986)

160

INSET 3.8 — TIPS FOR PROCRASTINATORS

1. Allow more time than you think a project will take. For example, if you think a writing assignment or report will take two hours, give yourself three or even four hours to do it.

2. Set realistic goals, but don't set them in stone. Stay flexible.

3. Break down big and intimidating projects into smaller, more doable ones.

4. Remove distractions from your workplace. Keep food, TV, magazines, games and other temptations out of your way.

5. Keep a list of backup projects — things you mean to do when you have time. Once you've made tips 1-9 part of your life, you will have the time to do them!

6. Plan to have fun without feeling guilty. Start with the things you enjoy most — the things you usually save for last and don't get around to at all. *Then* add the things you're supposed to do.

7. Reward yourself after each accomplishment, large or small.

8. Begin your day with your most difficult task. The rest of the day will seem easy by comparison.

9. Make a conscious effort to realize that your paper, project, or whatever can't be perfect. Accepting this helps deflate fear of a failure.

10. Keep a diary of your progress. List the things you accomplish each day. Read it over from time to time and feel proud of what you've done.

("10 Tips for Procrastinators" excerpt from *Perfectionism: What's Bad About Being Too Good* by Miriam Adderholdt-Elliott. Copyright © 1987. All rights reserved. Reprinted by permission of Free Spirit Publishing, Inc.)

161

Organizational Skills. Disorganization is a frequent symptom of Underachievement Syndrome. Most underachievers appear to be disorganized. For some, the disorganization shows itself in messy desks, messy papers and messy rooms. Others seem unable to plan their time and thus hand assignments in late or not at all. Concomitant with the disorganization patterns are statements which typically are not entirely honest, such as "I forgot," "I didn't know I had any homework," "I didn't know today was the deadline" or "I thought I had already completed the assignment." Although some students will admit that such statements are excuses, others will swear that the statements are honest and accurate. They seem like declarations of opposition to organization and commitments to nonconformity.

Two main parenting styles seem to foster disorganization patterns. One style is the family that advocates a disorganized lifestyle. They value disorganization as synonymous with freedom and creativity and assert openly that they prefer a disorganized lifestyle. The children thus emulate the parents and have never learned organizational techniques. Disorganization feels natural, right and creative and remains for the whole family a preferred approach to daily life. While it is true that many creative persons appear from the outside to live in disordered environments, it's in a sense an illusion. Creative persons aren't usually rigid and they do tolerate ambiguity well, but their real skill is in organizing chaos. They're frequently very detail oriented in their final product. Modeling organization strategies and allowing time for organizational tasks will be helpful to your children. Reasonable organizational strategies won't deter creativity and will enhance children's effective learning in school.

The second pattern is much more common and more difficult to identify. In this family situation, one parent uses disorganization as a passive aggressive power play in an oppositional marriage. One parent typically is a perfectionist, or very well-organized, and apparently the more powerful parent. The second parent can't assertively or rationally deal with his/her sense of powerlessness, so he/she uses passive aggressive techniques like forgetting things, not preparing things on time, not accomplishing tasks requested and ignoring responsibilities. Although this spouse feels powerless, he/she may be viewed as powerful by one or more of the children. Those children will emulate the passive aggressive parent in opposing the demanding, more structured parent. Disorganization relative to schoolwork becomes the power weapon for the child.

Living with a small amount of chaos or tolerance of ambiguity seems healthy and may contribute to creativity and a noncompulsive lifestyle. On the other hand, rigidity and perfectionism are likely to interfere with school and life achievement. Reasonable structure and organization are necessary to school and life accomplishment, and it appears again that moderation is more effective than extremism. Parents must take the initiative to model and teach reasonable organizational techniques as they relate to home and school responsibilities.

Children should always be advised to adopt techniques for remembering assignments. Model list making for organizing your own memory and advise children to adapt or make up a technique to reinforce their memory for school responsibilities (see Inset 3.9).

Anxieties and Disabilities

Your children may have deficits in basic skills which
cause you some real concerns. When a child has a
deficit in a particular skill, the parents are often asked
to help children practice. The effect of parents tutoring children in a skill is almost always disasterous. All
parents who work with their children in a deficient area
will feel considerable anxiety. The result will be that
your anxiety will convey itself to your child on a daily
basis. I was first alerted to this by a fourth-grade boy

who said, "How come my mom gets so tense when I read to her?" Insisting that a child read aloud to a parent is a daily lesson in reading anxiety. A parent teaching a child who is having problems with math provides a daily lesson in math anxiety. Taking learning out of an anxiety mode is a high priority.

Diagnostic tutoring in mathematics by an outside tutor will permit that tutor to sort out whether your child has difficulty understanding mathematics or whether math deficits are related to anxiety. If the latter is the case, goal-directed tutoring in mathematics will probably be sufficient to relieve the student's anxiety. That is, once these children have proven that they can catch-up in skills, they will have built sufficient confidence to go on independently. Tutoring should be temporary for these students or they will become dependent on the one-to-one instruction. Tutoring shouldn't be done by either a parent or sibling. The tutoring should stop as soon as children feel "caught up," but they should be encouraged to let you know, should they continue to want occasional help.

For writing anxieties, word processing and "speeding" exercises are sufficient to enhance confidence (see Inset 3.10). Dramatic improvement has been demonstrated repeatedly by use of computers. Children may use simple word processing programs by second grade and should be encouraged to do as much written work on the computer as possible. Don't require them to learn keyboarding first. Don't require that they rough draft right before they keyboard. They become further barriers. Let them learn keyboarding any way they prefer and write directly on the computer. Word processors give children a wonderful sense of control over their writing.

Many dependent children write slowly. It is impossible to determine the chicken/egg relationship here, whether slow writing encourages parental attention to dependency or dependent children write slower because they are less confident. Nevertheless, increasing writing speed is a goal worth pursuing. This can be accomplished using a personal self-completion model and can be applied to copying verbal written material or to doing math facts. The necessary materials include a digital watch and multiple sheets of the same math facts or written material to copy. Children copy the first material and set a baseline time which can be recorded on an old calendar. The next day they again write the same material and mark their time. For each time they beat their earlier time and write the material in fewer minutes or seconds, they earn five points on their chart; otherwise they receive only two points they normally would receive. Writing the same material every day may get boring, but they will soon find that they can write much faster. The selections they choose for writing should be shorter or longer depending on their age and can be varied every week or two.

The same approach can be used for speeding math fact knowledge. Begin with easier facts and do the same page for a whole week. Many dependent children become very tense during classroom timed tests. They will become much more relaxed about timed tests if timing themselves becomes a daily habit.

Reading anxiety is exemplified by children who rush through reading and guess at words based on ititial consonants and contextual clues. They don't have the confidence to sound words out phonetically. The following recommendations will help these children at home and school. These recommendations can do no harm even if your child is dyslexic.

1. Don't require children to read aloud to parents at home. The parents' anxiety conveys itself to the child. Children should read aloud only if they choose to do so. As adult readers, they will rarely find oral reading important.

2. Permit your children to stay up one half hour later at night if they're in their bed reading to themselves (they don't like to go to sleep; it's parents who do).

3. Encourage them to read whatever they like during that special time. Don't insist they read at grade level. Comics, cartoons, sports magazines, easy material and repeating books are all fine for building confidence. If they love reading they will expand their interests as their reading improves.

4. Read aloud to children as long as the experience is positive (eighth grade is not too old).

5. Encourage your children to read stories while listening to tapes of the stories.

6. Model reading by turning the television off and reading for your own pleasure.

7. Encourage your children to read to younger siblings, provided those siblings aren't good readers. This shouldn't be done in your presence.

Some children actually have learning disabilities. Inset 3.11 compares learning-disabled children to dependent underachievers.

Our general guiding rule for dealing with learning-disabled children is to attempt to help find them a nonperson-dependent adaptation to compensate for their disability. Thus, word processors and tape recorders are appropriate for children with writing disabilities. Shortened assignments are appropriate where extensive writing could be a laborious task. Teachers may be helpful with that adjustment.

Permitting children to dictate materials or stories to a teacher or parent would be inappropriate except in the case of very young children, since that would

INSET 3.11 — WAYS TO DISCRIMINATE BETWEEN DEPENDENCE AND DISABILITY

Dependence	Disability
1. Child asks for explanations regularly despite differences in subject matter.	Child asks for explanation in particular subjects which are difficult.
2. Child asks for explanation of instructions regardless of style used, either auditory or visual.	Child asks for explanation of instructions only when given in one instruction style, either auditory or visual, but not both.
3. Child's questions are not specific to material but appear to be mainly to gain adult attention.	Child's questions are specific to material and once process is explained child works efficiently.
4. Child is disorganized or slow in assignments but becomes much more efficient when a meaningful reward is presented as motivation.	Child's disorganization or slow pace continues despite motivating rewards.
5. Child works only when an adult is nearby at school and/or at home.	Child works independently once process is clearly explained.
6. Individually administered measures of ability indicate that the child is capable of learning the material. Individual tests improve with tester encouragement and support. Group measures may not indicate good abilities or skills.	Both individual and group measures indicate lack of specific abilities or skills. Tester encouragement has no significant effect on scores.

Dependence	Disability
7. Child exhibits "poor me" body language (tears, helplessness, pouting, copying) regularly when new work is presented. Teacher or adult attention serves to ease the symptoms.	Child exhibits "poor me" body language only with instructions or assignments in specific disability areas and accepts challenges in areas of strength.
8. Parents report whining, complaining, attention getting, temper tantrums and poor sportsmanship at home.	Although parents may find similar symptoms at home, they tend to be more sporadic than regular, particularly the whining and complaining.
9. Child's "poor me" behavior appears only with one parent and not with the other; only with some teachers and not with others. With some teachers or with the other parent the child functions fairly well independently.	Although the child's "poor me" behaviors may only appear with one parent or with solicitous teachers, performance is not adequate even when behavior is acceptable.
10. Child learns only when given one-to-one instruction but will not learn in groups even when instructional mode is varied.	Although child may learn more quickly in a one-to-one setting, he/she will also learn efficiently in a group setting provided the child's disability is taken into consideration when instructions are given.

It is critical to realize that some children who are truly disabled have also become dependent. The key to distinguishing between disability and dependence is the child's response to adult support. If the child performs only with adult support when new material is presented he/she is too dependent, whether or not there is also a disability.

(Rimm, 1986)

encourage person dependency. Dictating tests to children or their dictating answers to teachers also encourages dependency.

In the same way, reading while listening to a tape recording of subject content material will be helpful and could even facilitate reading skills. Expecting to have adults reading required lessons to children would maintain person-dependent patterns and is not a good idea.

A small number of students who come to our Clinic seem to exhibit a spatial disability. Low scores on Block Design and Object Assembly of the WISC-R* are characteristic of these children. Schoolwork which seems especially difficult includes telling time, use of money, geometry, math story problems, maps and geography, math-related science and diagrams.

We have recommended the following games and activities to enhance spatial skills. They can be played at home or at school. However, don't be surprised if your children with spatial disabilities aren't fond of these activities. They tend to find them difficult. Thus, a few minutes a day may be all you should expect. Try to keep them "fun" so children's anxiety doesn't increase. Games and activities include the following: puzzles, Legos, blocks, TV games, Tangrams, cards (War, Go Fish, etc.), concentration, dominoes, checkers, chess, Chinese checkers, Monopoly, money games and board games.

Practice in the Arts

The purpose for most children, of providing music or dance lessons is to give them exposure to learning in the arts. We assume that if they learn to love and appreciate music or dance by their involvement that

*Wechsler Intelligence Scale for Children — Revised (1974)

171

they will appreciate those arts, either as part of their recreational enrichment activities or as a member of an appreciative audience when they become adults. For a very few of your children you may believe that they are sufficiently talented in the arts to develop a career in their area of talent. Whether you see music as an opportunity for enrichment or as a career will make a difference in the kinds of opportunities you will want to encourage and in the expectations you'll have for your children. Although most parents want their children to love music, a visitor from an outside planet who observed music practice time in most families, would surely assume that the real purpose of music was to teach Mother how to improve her expertise in nagging and to teach children to improve their arguing techniques. Hardly ever do we find families where the "practice battle" doesn't take place on a regular basis. Although the parents' original assumption was that children would enjoy music and that children want to take music lessons, only rarely do parents proceed based on that assumption.

I'm a firm believer in encouraging musical opportunities for children. However, I'm also a firm believer in parents remembering the purpose of music lessons. Although the music teachers of the world seem to have joined together to proclaim that children must practice a minimum of one half hour a day, the parents must unite and tell the music teachers of the world that one half hour isn't on their agenda or that of their children. Do you remember when you were a child and had to practice for half an hour of piano, trumpet or ballet or whatever art form your lessons involved? Do you remember how you practiced the first ten minutes, stared out the window, made silly noises, looked at the clock, wasted a few minutes here or there and then went back

to practicing a few more minutes? Do you recall how you manufactured ways to fill up that half hour like, "I have to go to the bathroom" or "My nose is running" or "I forgot my book in the other room?" Children haven't changed much in their abilities to fill up the required half hour by procrastinating and avoiding practice.

I'd suggest that when your children request music lessons that you negotiate the number of minimum times they'll play a piece and ask that they make a commitment to that. For example, if they're playing piano, they should promise to play a particular piece four or five times each day they practice. If they select a number for practices, they're less likely to rehearse their avoidance talents and more likely to fulfill their agreement.

After you've negotiated with them the number of times they'll play their pieces, the next important recommendation is that you leave practice to them. Don't make it your parenting responsibility. As they begin their lessons, negotiate a three-month agreement indicating that if they handle their practice responsibly for three months, then they may continue with their lessons. Tell them that if they prefer not to practice, after three months, you'll be happy to discontinue their lessons. Indicate that you'll be willing to give them another opportunity at a later time when they feel more ready to practice on their own. If children do continue to take responsibility for their practice, even though it may be a more limited practice than their teachers would prefer, you'll find that as they achieve higher levels in their music, they'll be willing to increase their practice. They'll be motivated by their intrinsic interest, preparations for concerts and contests, or by their relationship to an inspiring teacher. Mature levels of performance in the arts aren't accomplished by punishment or parent nagging.

If you, as parents, would like to do something to encourage your children's music, you may want to set aside time for family concerts for your children. Establishing Friday night as children's performance night and inviting aunts, uncles or grandparents might be fun. Weekly concerts or a concert every two or three weeks may motivate children to prepare their favorite pieces. The brief concerts can be formalized and made a bit more credible by children announcing their pieces, earning some applause, and after the recital, serving cookies and tea. As they mature, school, state and national contests will take over as performance motivators.

Parenting so that children will learn includes learning about the arts. However, as in other routines and habits, encouraging children to take responsibility, moving your positive attention to their accomplishment and giving them support for carrying through their practice independently, will encourage them to enjoy music or dance performance.

Morning, Noon and Night

You may wonder why routines that describe waking up in the morning, eating meals, and putting children to bed at night would be included under habits and routines for *How To Parent So Children Will Learn*. Imagine children who are awakened by parents in the morning half a dozen times, scolded to get up, nagged to get dressed, nagged to eat breakfast, nagged to get their school books ready and nagged to get out to the bus. As these children enter school, they have already incorporated a nag-dependent pattern. They feel negative about themselves and have learned that other people will take responsibility for them. That pattern will be generalized into the classroom and these

175

children will expect teachers to take responsibilities for them throughout their day. So home nagging generalizes to school nagging and that's why morning, meal and night routines are incorporated into this book.

Morning Routine. Routines are more effective if a point of accountability is established. For example, the point at which your children are held accountable for morning responsibilities is at breakfast. They don't eat breakfast until their morning obligations are met.

Be as positive as possible when you explain these routines. For example, "I'm looking forward to breakfast together" is a better statement than, "If you don't do your chores there is no breakfast." Parents and children may make a list of morning responsibilities together and hang them on the mirror as a reminder. Some children may even prefer checklists and preschoolers who don't read may use pictorial reminders. The establishing of these routines moves the responsibility from parent (nagging) to children. Insets 3.12 and 3.13 give examples of bad and good morning routines.

INSET 3.12 — DEPENDENT MORNING ROUTINE

Mom: Bobby, are you up?

Bobby: (No answer)

Mom: Bobby, it's time to get up!

Bobby: Um - awfully tired - a few more minutes.

Mom: Bobby, you better get up, you'll miss the bus! (Repeated with increasing volume 3 to 10 times)

That's only the beginning. Admonitions to wash face, brush teeth, eat breakfast, hurry, wear different clothes, remember lunch money, school books, notes and finally warnings about the soon-to-arrive school bus or parent pickup add to the unrelinquishing din. Arguments between siblings on bathroom use, clothes exchange and breakfast choices punctuate the distressing beginning of the day. If two parents are awake, interparent debate about the degree of nagging reinforces the hassled start of each new morning.

(Rimm, 1986)

INSET 3.13 — "HOW TO" - FRESH MORNING START!

Step 1:   Announce to your children the guidelines for the new beginning. From this day forth they will be responsible for getting themselves ready for school. Your job will be to await them at the breakfast table for a pleasant morning chat.

Step 2:   Night before preparations include the laying out of their clothes, getting their books ready in the book bag and setting the alarm early enough to allow plenty of morning time. They will feel just as tired at 7 a.m. as they will at 6:30, but the earlier start will prevent their usual rush. The purchase of a new alarm clock may usher in the new routine. Children as young as four may use their own alarm clock.

Step 3:   They wake themselves up (absolutely no calls from others), wash, dress and pick up their room (as itemized in checklist). Breakfast comes only when they are ready for school. Absolutely no nagging!

Step 4:   A pleasant family breakfast and conversation about the day ahead! Parent *waits* at the breakfast table and is not anywhere around them prior to their meal together.

INSET 3.13 — "HOW TO" - FRESH MORNING START!
(continued)

Question: What happens if they don't dress in time for breakfast?

Answer: No breakfast. (That will only happen two or three times for children who like to eat.)

Question: What happens if my children don't like to eat breakfast?

Answer: Fifteen minutes of cartoons after breakfast, when they're ready for school will probably be effective.

Question: What happens if they don't get up?

Answer: They miss school and stay in their room all day. That will happen no more than once.

Question: What happens if they don't have enough time in the morning?

Answer: They go to bed 30 minutes earlier and set the alarm 30 minutes earlier until they find the right amount of time necessary for independent mornings.

Question: What happens if I have to drive them to school or day-care on the way to work?

Answer: Insist that they are in your car on time, in whatever state they are, when you're ready to go. They may finish dressing in the car or on the bus. Stay calm. They'll get the idea.

Question: Does this routine work?

Answer: Always with elementary-aged children. Sometimes with high school students. Never with high school students who like to skip school.

Meal Routines. Difficulties during meals are often inspired by negative bids for attention. If mealtime behavior is inappropriate, timing your children out until after the meal is effective. They may then eat the **cold** meal **alone**. Don't feel sorry for them. You needn't feel at all guilty since a meal awaits them. Even if they skipped a meal, they wouldn't starve (contrary to the belief of some parents). When expectations are established for proper behavior at family mealtime, behavior will improve. Continued negative power struggles over eating are much more harmful than occasional "time-outs." Be calm, but not picky. Dessert and evening snacks come only after a reasonable meal is consumed. These old-fashioned rewards are still effective.

Sometimes picky eaters have arrived at their pickiness because parents have given them too many choices and too much power. After all, many of us think of food as love, so parents are concerned that their children are not deprived of food or love. Here are a few illustrative cases:

Case 1

Miriam was 6 months old. As her grandmother (me) fed her cereal, Miriam moved her head to the side. Grandmom's spoon followed. Miriam led. Grandmom followed. "Why?" thought Grandmom to herself. "I'm not hungry, she is." New design. Grandmom stopped following and just held the spoon. Miriam was hungry and Miriam ate. Miriam stopped turning her head. That game wasn't working. Notice that the age mentioned was 6 months.

Case 2

Benjy liked peanut butter sandwiches. Mother gave the children choices for lunch. Benjy ate peanut butter sandwiches daily. However, dinner had a more prescribed and well-balanced menu. One day Benjy tried peanut butter power. "Mom," he asked, "I don't like ravioli. How about if I make a peanut butter sandwich?" Mom thought that was better than arguing and it was Benjy's choice. Soon, Benjy chose peanut butter sandwiches two days a week, then three days.

Mom got the idea and she announced to Benjy one day, "I'm afraid you'll turn into a peanut butter sandwich, so I'm changing the choices. At lunch, you choose. At dinner, I choose. At lunch, it can be peanut butter. At dinner, it's whatever everyone eats or nothing." That precipitated a bit of anger and a few time-outs. Benjy got the idea and after a few weeks of battle, discovered that there was more to dinner than peanut butter.

Fussy eaters come into being by having been given too many choices. It's natural for children to want to eat. It's only when we educate them to play power games with food that meals become problem times.

Try to keep mealtime pleasant. Give children and adults reasonable choices, but you don't have to become a short-order cook or cater to your children's power whims. They can have more options when you take them to a restaurant.

Bedtime. Many children are extraordinarily talented in the skill of avoiding bedtime. Somehow that talent disappears by parenthood and you're thus left with a situation where you find yourselves more tired than

your children each evening. If your children's bedtime avoidance talent exceeds your ability to stay awake, you'll find yourselves without any private adult time. This delayed bedtime produces tired children during the day and discontented partners in a marriage. Reasonable and consistent bedtimes produce happier adults and, hopefully, more alert, intelligent children.

While there's no exact time for children to be in bed and their sleep needs may vary with their energy level, these suggestions may guide you for school nights. Be flexible enough to consider their energy level but firm enough to provide yourself with some adult time.

Grades K - 2: 7:00 - 8:00
3 - 6: 7:30 - 9:00
7 - 12: 9:00 - 10:00

For that last group, particularly in senior high school, the ten o'clock guideline would mean that they must be in their room, although not necessarily asleep.

If you follow the routine described in Inset 3.14, you'll find getting children to sleep a pleasant ritual instead of a battle.

Bedtime fears may become an issue only if you let them. Certainly don't let them become an avoidance technique. If children are afraid or worried about ghosts, permit them to leave a hall light or night-light on. A way for them to handle their fears without becoming dependent on a parent is important. That means that you don't go to sleep with them at night or tuck them into your bed or permit them to sleep on the living room sofa. It also means that you don't spend a lot of time discussing their fears. A night-light will serve well to dispel all ghosts and when they feel ready to be brave they can turn it off.

Sometimes very young children trap parents into rocking them or carrying them around until they fall asleep. That **used** to be called spoiling a child. It still **is** spoiling the child. Of course, there's nothing wrong with comforting or holding a child when they aren't well. All children should have plenty of hugs and cuddling. However, falling asleep on a regular basis is something they should learn to do independently. That means you, as parents, will probably have to permit your children to cry themselves to sleep once or twice. That's usually all it takes, although some children are more resistant. It's harder on you, as parents, than on your children. Blankets, stuffed animals, or anything else that comforts them is fine, but when the responsibility for falling asleep becomes yours or your spouse's, then you do have a spoiled child. If you have a baby that cries once in awhile at bedtime, they probably need comfort. If they cry regularly, you probably need the comfort and the permission to let your baby cry him or herself to sleep.

INSET 3.14 — BEDTIME ROUTINE

1. Bedtime becomes less stressful for everyone if a night routine is set up for children. Our children used to call it their "ceremonies." That framework permits children to expect bedtime and avoids their making it into a nightly exercise in avoidance. If there's a reasonably regular structure, children actually respond more flexibly to exceptions.

2. To establish a bedtime routine, make a list with your children of prebedtime tasks. For example, the list might include bath, dress in pajamas, get books ready for school next day, take clothes out for next day, etc. Ask them to tape the list to their mirror or wall. The final activities of the list might be snack, parent reading, chatting time and quiet reading to themselves in bed. The last three can vary with family preferences and age. Some parents don't like to provide a bedtime snack. Some parents may prefer to stop reading to children eventually, although it's appropriate as long as it remains an enjoyable activity. Some children will stay up all night reading to themselves if no time limit is given.

3. Now ask your children to follow their list and be sure that you don't nag them through it. The last parts, snacks, story time, etc. are dependent on whether the first are accomplished on time. When you explain this to your children, please be positive. Don't threaten. Just say, for example, "hurry and do all the things on the list so we can have more time for reading tonight."

4. Once children have completed their ceremonies, explain that they *must* stay in their own rooms. If they insist on calling to you every few minutes or coming out to interrupt you, warn them once that if that continues you'll have to close and latch their door until they fall asleep. Assure them that you'll open it once they're asleep. Usually the warning is enough for them to know that you're serious, but for some children you may want to use that latch once or twice. If they're frightened they may leave a light on. Your intention is not to punish, but to set a definite limit.

5. Be sure to make exceptions for special occasions, weekends or summer. Children respect fair rules better than rigid ones. However, do **enforce** the bedtime rules regularly for their sake and your own.

Chores and Work. One of the the most frequent complaints I hear from parents is "they never make their bed." Making beds is clearly a symbol of children's rebellion against chores. I recall as a child wondering why my own mother put so much value on getting my bed made. As I listen with concern to the "unmade bed" symptom described by so many parents, I find myself wondering about the state of my own bed for the day. Whether or not I managed to hastily arrange the covers and spread varies with the time of my first commitments of the day and my last appointments the night before. I never feel great concern for my client's unmade bed; I know that children and parents will survive that degree of disorganization. However, if your children don't assist with home responsibilities willingly and aren't required to maintain their own rooms to at least minimal standards, then I believe that home responsibilities are a problem. For example:

> Bobby said, "I believe I have a right to have my own room exactly as I like it, and I prefer the mess."

> Bobby's parents concluded, initially, that he should be allowed this freedom. However, they soon began feeling concerned. He slept without sheets rather than make his bed. Crumbs all over the floor attracted ants. He picked up his laundry only when he was out of clothes, and he stopped inviting friends to their home because he was ashamed of his room.

> Bobby's room had progressed beyond reasonableness. So had his schoolwork. His parents kept a very neat household. His father was a perfectionist; his mother was passive aggressive. In response to her husband's power,

Bobby, in symbolic rebellion with his mother, determined to hold his room as a bastion of power (and mess).

The younger children in our Clinic are treated to a series of group therapy sessions in which we spend at least one session on family cooperative effort. A song which delights them all from the musical *Free To Be You and Me* (Harnick, 1972), is one which acknowledges that those "ladies on TV" who smile when they're doing housework are actresses and are paid for those commercials. Further, it points out that everybody, including Mom and Dad, hates housework. In the final appeal of the song it says:

Little boys, little girls,
When you are big husbands and wives,
If you want all the days of your lives
To seem sunny as summer weather,
Make sure when there is housework to do
That you do it together.

The song is followed in therapy by asking that children devise ways in which they can be of help. We introduce cooperative statements which they've rarely used but which have been a humorous standby at our own home. "Sure, Mom, I'll be glad to" or "sure, Dad, I'll be glad to" take on special meaning when family members attack some of our more odious tasks like retarring the blacktop or mopping up the flooded basement floor. They surpass "do I have to?" or "why doesn't John have to do the hard work that I have to?" The song and the discussion send children out of our therapy sessions offering to do household tasks, to the surprise of their parents. However, I wouldn't dare collect data on the continuity of their willingness. Parents do need to cultivate and even insist on a sharing of household responsibilities.

How to do it? It isn't easy! These tasks are not all fun, but really must be done. Again, personal attention is your most powerful reinforcer. You can best teach your children good work habits in one-to-one partnerships. If they share a job with you or your spouse, you model the skills, show your appreciation for their cooperation, and give them a sense of importance and self-confidence that come from completing a difficult task. If you can establish that pattern early, they'll be willing coworkers and will eventually move toward independence. Early parent patience results in cultivating good work habits and perseverance. While you're working as an adult-child team, don't let the child quit until the job's complete.

Giving two siblings a task to share is their invitation to compete. Either they will compete to make one the "worker" and the other the "shirker," or they will vie for who can get away with the least work. Don't expect motivation or cooperation. Sibling chore efforts have a hidden agenda. Getting away with as little as possible is the typical goal. Even when you, as parents, work in a partnership with your children, you'll find that they are all more effective if you work with one at a time, at least until they know how to be effective workers. Here's a case example:

> David and Scott were three years apart and David, the older boy, was an underachiever, while Scott, the younger of the two, was achieving well in school and appeared to be positive and well-adjusted. When I asked David how he felt about work, his response was, "I hate work." I asked him if he meant all kinds of work and he was adamant in pointing out that he meant all kinds of work; schoolwork or work around the house. I asked him if he ever did work with his dad and he

said, "Yes," and he hated that as well. I further asked him did he recall he had ever done work with his dad without his brother around? He thought about that for a few seconds and responded by saying, "Yes, I did work with my dad once all by myself and I really did enjoy that."

What quantity and quality of work do you insist on? Do you pay for chores accomplished? Please don't expect your own personal standards of excellence; something below what you'd expect for yourself is reasonable and fair. Regarding payment, paying children for working is debatable and optional. Certainly some tasks should be done without salary as part of family responsibility. If you do pay them, use children's standards for salary. (Too much money is more than they can manage.) Savings accounts are a good and positive diversion for their funds. It's a good idea to invent some special jobs as a means for children to earn some money. They may require some extra funds for Christmas or birthdays and you may enjoy having them wash the kitchen floor.

Mom and Dad, avoid getting into a nagging mode. Two reminders are enough. Beyond that, children aren't listening. Use a written checklist and clear consistent consequences. For example, rooms can have Friday inspections before weekend activities are permitted. If rooms are clean, they go out. If not, they stay home until their room meets preassigned standards. As children develop reasonably good and regular habits, such consequences and inspections won't be necessary, but you may want to use them to get the responsibilities started. Most important, stay with the promised negative consequences if tasks aren't completed. They can be removed immediately upon completion.

Children may resist at first, but parent persistence pays off in reasonable, responsible behavior. Teaching your children to be effective workers is an important component of teaching them to be persevering learners.

Why Do We Do It? Why Do We Nag?

Why do we do for children what they could do for themselves? Why do we take on their responsibilities and then remind them dozens of times that the responsibilities are theirs? Why do we worry so at their slightest discomfort, the possibility that they might not eat enough or sleep enough? Why are we concerned that they they will not feel loved when we love them so?

Sigmund Freud (1959) described the infant as ruled by the pleasure principle that demanded immediate gratification and Erikson (1963) described the necessity of infants accomplishing the developmental task of trust during the first year of life. As parents, we define our role as meeting our infants needs so that they may trust us and intuitively feel that they are loved. Immediate gratification of our children's needs gets defined as love.

Out of love we may rock them, nag them, overfeed them, do their homework for them, study for them, learn for them and work for them. All these we do immediately to satisfy their needs. In so doing, we steal from them their initiative, their confidence and their ability to delay gratification. Yet, children's learning to postpone gratification is an important predictor of cognitive and social competence later in life (Mischel, Shoda & Rodriguez, 1989).

Can it be that loving our children so much is what gets us in trouble? No, not exactly. It isn't the loving, but it is our concern with demonstrating our love immediately. We do what makes our children feel good at the moment, instead of thinking about the "big picture." Thus, we teach them to demand from us immediate gratification and they become habituated to it. If we can learn to wait patiently while they learn, then we can teach them patience, perseverance and independence. A "now" generation is not an achievement-motivated generation.

Fun and Games

You may wonder why I include Fun and Games under Habits and Routines that support learning. As I think back to our own children's growing up, I recall with the most nostalgia the times of family game playing, the smell of popcorn, the humor, the joking, the competition, that sense of kidding, winning and losing, accepting challenge that took place during game playing. Game playing is relevant to learning and relevant to life. When children do homework or chores, in addition to the intrinsic motivation that comes from the experience of accomplishment, there should be a motivation that's based on the realization that after the work is over, there's time for fun.

Family game playing is also a good exercise in learning to compete. Humor helps children to cope with the losing. Don't give a lot of attention to poor losers. Label it "poor sportsmanship," ignore the loser, and go on with the fun of the game. If it seems to dependent children that they've missed fun by withdrawing, they'll soon rejoin you. Permit them to do that without a lot of attention or explanation and they'll soon forget their sadness. Absolutely don't persuade; that makes it difficult for children to rejoin without losing face.

Game playing should always be designed as fair competition. That may mean you should give children a handicap, but don't ever just let them win. That takes away their sense of control and teaches them to depend on winning for fun. Learning the balance between winning and losing is the goal. Any time winning is fixed before the game is played, it invalidates teaching competition. Games encourage children toward risk taking by providing a safe environment in which they can compete with family members. Games will help children build confidence. The absolute "don'ts" are:

1. Don't just let them win.

2. Don't feel sorry for them or overreact when they lose.

3. Don't pay a lot of attention to their being afraid to try.

4. Don't let their avoiding competition keep the rest of the family from having fun.

5. Humor and laughter go a long way.

Make time for family fun and games! Outdoor play, camping experiences, bicycling, sports, indoor board games or throwing a Nerf basketball into a basket hung on the side of the door all qualify as possibilities.

The family that surrounds itself with family fun and laughter is more likely to motivate its children to learn, work and accomplish. The game playing and fun should be as much a habit as the homework and chores. That habit is probably harder for parents than it is for children. So I ask you, as parents, to try to accomplish this most difficult habit of all, despite your own sense of overload. Have fun!

4

How to Model and Expect Achievement

If you loved school and enjoy your adult work, you are potentially an ideal role model for your children's love of learning. If neither work nor school or only one has been good for you, prepare for some playacting. Haven't you always wanted to try a little theater? Here's your opportunity.

How to Model Achievement

Children copy much of what they see. For better or for worse, they watch you and copy you.

You Are Their Models. Three main variables cause a child to copy or imitate an adult: (1) similarities between the child and the adult, (2) nurturance or a special warmth that's felt between the child and the adult, and (3) power as perceived by the child (Mussen & Rutherford, 1963; Hetherington & Frankie, 1967). You can probably intentionally increase your children's unconscious copying of their parents' and their teachers' achievement-oriented behaviors if you describe their parents and their teachers in achieving ways. A secondary benefit is that a "self-fulfilling prophecy" operates to improve that achieving attitude of those you describe.

How Do You Like Your Work? Children can't copy you when they don't see you. If they don't see you at work, they can't copy your activities on the job. You may be terrific in the workplace. That will not affect them. However, when you arrive at home, your description and your spouse's description of your jobs, provide a model for how your children may feel about work. How do you walk into the house? What do you say? Here are some typical examples:

I'm exhausted - another impossible day at work!

My boss is horrible. I really must find another job.

Twenty more years until retirement! Do you think I'll ever make it?

The more I do, the more they expect.

Could anything be more pressured than my work?

Did you make the bed, buy the groceries, do the laundry? You can't expect me to do everything. I'm working 50 hours a week. (So much for women's liberation.)

I'd like to go on strike. No one appreciates me anyway.

I could earn more on unemployment.

Fifteen years of education and I hate my job.

Why don't you get a different job? Yours isn't worth the hassle.

Medicine sure isn't what it used to be?

All these comments emerge from adults who are successful in their careers. Imagine what children might hear if their parents were failures or if they were out of work?

How Was School Today? Your son or daughter walks in from school. You ask, when you get home, "How was school today?" They go for the food, turn on the television, grunt and respond:

Terrible. It was boring.

My teacher expects too much.

The teacher's always yelling.

More homework. Work, work, work.

Boring, boring, boring!

And your responses to these "enthusiastic" children:

I don't know what's wrong with teachers these days.

School was pretty boring for me too.

All you ever do is complain.

I don't know why we pay all those taxes.

Teachers put too much pressure on kids.

I wish they'd challenge you instead of giving you all that "busywork."

Dan, an eighth grader, responded to my question about which parent he was the most the same as in this surprising way. "I guess I'm like my mom because she doesn't really want to work but she wants more money. I don't want to work, but I'd like all *As.*" He was hearing a message from a hardworking mom that she didn't realize she was giving.

Change the Work Script. Home is your support system. It's a safe place where you should be able to say what you feel. If your children are listening and copying, perhaps it's time to give a more balanced view. We'll allow you 20 percent of the time for griping. Eighty percent is the usual competency standard. Put a smile on your face and try these for a change of script:

It's been a hard day, but a good day.

I really helped someone today.

My education really paid off. I'm doing a job I enjoy.

This may not be an ideal job, but I'm learning.

I guess you have to pay your dues. I don't mind doing a little extra.

Let me tell you about my interesting day.

It feels good to make a difference.

Of course, no one expects you to lie about your work to your children. If you've done a good day's work, you're likely to be tired. That's all right and expected. Try to get beyond your low energy level to describe your accomplishments. That will have a remarkably positive

impact on your children, your spouse and even on your own personal attitude about your work. It's not really an act, but it is a more balanced script.

If you've changed your work script, your children's school script may already have begun to change. They do truly copy their parents, their teachers, their friends and any other people whom they value and observe.

Change the School Script. Children's attitudes about teachers and school will improve if you change your descriptions of their teachers and your former teachers. Try these positive script modifications:

Teachers really have a hard job. They must really care about kids.

I remember my fifth-grade teacher. She/he was really special. I even remember what I learned.

Study can really be boring. But there's that good feeling that comes when you really know your stuff.

I bet that teacher doesn't realize you'd like a challenge. Why don't I talk to him/her about that?

I have some really good memories of school.

Some of the things I never thought would be useful turned out to really help me.

Specific descriptions of incidents will help make your own positive school experiences real to your children. Some parents devote all their school descriptions to what they got away with, how they avoided working, how terrible their teachers were or what a waste of time school was. Instead, pick and choose the

positive experiences that really made the best differences in your education. Don't lie and tell them everything was wonderful, but do give a balanced view which focuses on your good school experiences. There really were a lot of them. It will be good for you and good for your children to recall those positive stories together.

Designing an Achiever Image. Since parent modeling of achievement is so important to children's learning, you'll want to act as appropriate role models. Not only should you be achieving persons, but you must share with your children a realistic and positive view of achievement. They should learn from you the ways in which efforts and outcomes are related. They must understand that you sometimes fail, but that you survive that failure, persevere, and succeed again. They should view both your creativity and your conformity. They should understand the intrinsic and extrinsic rewards that come with your efforts. There should be some balance of the positive and negative in their view of you as achieving models. If you're an achiever, that balance probably exists, but sometimes parents unintentionally show a biased and only negative perspective to their children.

You should also design an "achiever image" of your spouse. Here are some common pitfalls of which to be aware. Mother may complain continually about her husband's frequent work. She may say, "I wish Dad wouldn't have to work so hard. He has no time to be with the family." Sometimes she describes Dad's career as terrible or blames his loss of temper on his job. She may attribute family problems to her husband's boss or blame his work for their marriage or economic problems.

To avoid these pitfalls, you should interpret to your children the financial and life satisfaction benefits of your husband's hard work. Although you may be honest about the parts of his career that you don't value, you must also emphasize the positive components of that career and explain why Dad chose it. (Remember, at least 80% of the time.)

In some circumstances it may seem either extremely difficult or else very trivial to build up Dad's career. However, once you see the parallel between your spouse's achievement at work and your children's achievement attitude at school, you'll be convinced. The mother who engages in continual tirades about her husband's awful career must be prepared to hear similar attitudes about school from her children. By adolescence, she's likely to find the comments quite intolerable. They sound like this:

I don't see why I have to do all this schoolwork; I need time for fun.

I'm not anything like my dad and I'd never choose a career like his.

I don't know what I want to do or be; something where I don't have to work all the time.

The bad grades aren't my fault; that teacher is terrible; he expects too much.

For every message Mother has given about her spouse, there will be a similar communication delivered by her children about school, because school is the child's workplace. There may be times in your married life where it's indeed impossible to avoid negativism and pessimism. However, if mothers can learn to provide a more positive and balanced view of

their husband's career, they can certainly expect more positive attitudes about school achievement in their children.

Fathers share the same kind of responsibility for describing their wife's work, whether it's a career outside the home or homemaking. However, the pitfalls are somewhat different. The common problem that fathers have is that they tend to devalue their wife's contributions. Comments like, "Didn't you do anything today?" or "All you ever do is run around and shop" (as the family sits down to a delicious home-cooked dinner in their mother-cleaned home in their mother-laundered clothes) puts the unsalaried homemaker into a category of "lazy." Volunteer activities, which take effort, creativity and responsibility and may make important contributions to the community or to the children, are often described by father as a "waste of time."

If Mother decides to return to school for further education, Father may describe that education as "busywork" or point out that Mom's schooling is interfering with the family meals and activities. This puts Mother's education (as well as education in general) in a nonessential, nonvalued perspective. If Mother begins a career later in life, because she has waited for the children to grow up, she may have a salary disadvantage related to her late start, her lesser training and experience, her geographic limitations or to the generally lower salaries paid to women. Some fathers minimize the financial contribution she makes as well as the lesser prestige of her job.

The main danger of Father's commentary is in the devaluing and depowering of his wife. Frequently his wife has the primary responsibility for disciplining the children, communicating with schools and providing educational guidance to the children (children don't

copy powerless models). Although Dad hasn't directly told his children not to obey their mother, he has,
in fact, modeled disrespect without being aware of the
seriousness of his communication. Not only has he
devalued his wife, but he's also underrated all that she
represents: caring for children empathically and lov-
ingly, concern with education and learning and the
tremendous initiative it takes to combine education
or career with homemaking. His children will view their
mother, at least partially, through his description. Boys
will ignore and put down this mother and may
underachieve. Girls will compete and argue with her
and may also underachieve. Dad should explicitly
describe his respect for his wife's efforts, contributions,
satisfactions and commitments to the community and
to education if he expects his children to achieve in
school and to respect their mother. (Mothers who see
me in our Clinic love this part of my recommendations.)

Modeling achievement and describing it in your
spouse make a critical difference in your children's
achievement motivation. If it sounds idealistic or impossible, listen to what your children are saying about
school. You'll know that they're watching you and
listening to you. They've received your messages about
your work and your spouse's work. If you expect them
to change their efforts and attitudes, you'll want to
change your modeling.

Parents, what I'm asking you to do on your home
stage, is to openly respect and support each other's
work. It's a hard act to dramatize in our pressured society. Let me share with you my humble attempts.

In the old days, when my first children were little,
it was expected that good mothers stayed home full
time to take care of their children. I tried to be a good
mother and did just that. So when Ilonna was born,

(she's 31 — I gave birth to her when I was eight), I stayed home with her and then started graduate school. Soon after I began, I became pregnant with David. I left graduate school and stayed at home with Ilonna and David until they were both in school and then returned for the second time to graduate school. Soon after I began, I became pregnant with Eric. I was beginning to think that pregnancy was somehow related to graduate school. Nevertheless, I waited until Eric was in kindergarten and returned for the third time. I was determined that my third return to graduate school would continue until my degree. But, sure enough, Sara was born. I didn't dare drop out again. I took two weeks from classes to give birth and returned to school.

You can understand that our older children were brought up in a very different parenting environment than our younger children.

While parenting Sara, I was always either at school or working part or full time. She learned early how to make her mother feel guilty. By age three, I recall her lying on the bed, looking up at the ceiling, as I worked on one of my interminable papers saying, "When I grow up I think I'll just be a mom." Do you think she was giving me a message? When I drove Sara to gymnastics, swimming or scouts, she would question, "How come you gave the other children more time than you give me?" Then from the back seat of our station wagon Eric or David would chime in, "We remember when you used to cook, Mom." For years, I apologized, and for years, I felt guilty. The guilt reminders only increased.

Finally, I determined it was time to change my response. When Sara would try to remind me of my motherly inadequacy, I would simply assure her that she was a lucky child to have such a good role model. I would tell her that I loved my work and was making my small contribution. I even convinced her that she was probably better off growing up as an independent "latchkey kid." To our back seat children, I reminded them that it wasn't too serious that we had to eat out occasionally. At least they could make choices. They were beginning to believe that *Red Barn* was home cooking. Their unpleasant comments diminished. My guilt decreased. My modeling act improved. I felt better.

When I would return home from my many hours at the Clinic, after speaking to adolescents or their parents most of the day, I faced a special challenge. My adolescent daughter awaited me impatiently. As I drove up our driveway, I would remind myself of the importance of my modeling to our daughter. At least some of the time I would walk into the house, place a smile on my face and say, "Did you have a good today, Sara?" And, sure enough, Sara was there to greet me with her good day. The sharing of our experiences, including those in the Clinic, were part of our evening conversation. She heard about my enthusiastic days, as well as about a few of my discouraging ones. Soon, Sara was thinking about majoring in psychology. She concluded, "I guess I was born into it." Indeed, my career was an important part of her life, and provided a positive sharing for both of us. Incidentally, Sara presently works with monkeys, not children. There is a similarity, you know.

When Parents Can't Control the Models (Or Can They?)

Children may copy many possible models in the process of growing up. They may identify with other relatives including grandparents, uncles, aunts, cousins or other siblings. They may copy stepparents or a birth parent from whom their other birth parent is divorced.

They may select teachers as models. Church leaders, scout leaders, music teachers and athletic or drama coaches are frequently selected as models by their students. Television and literature also provide models for children. Some are appropriate for encouraging their learning and some are grossly inappropriate. Finally, and not least of all, children and particularly adolescents will select peers as models. Most or many of these models can't be controlled by you, as parents. At least it feels that way. Here are some examples which provide suggestions for you, as parents, for encouraging your children's selections of appropriate role models and for influencing the models they've already selected.

Special Talent Teacher or Coach. When your children select role models who combine excellent qualities with problems, you'll want to communicate to those models carefully, so that you can reinforce the beneficial relationship while preventing the potential harm. The case of Kurt provides an example:

> Kurt was a talented violinist. His music teacher encouraged him and was an inspiration to him. As she shared her own musical career and her musical experience with Kurt, she provided him with messages of his competence that inspired him to many hours of practice and self-discipline. She served as an appropriate role model for his musical dedication. However, at some point in a conference with Kurt, after he described his failing grades in science and math, subjects in which he was also extremely talented, his teacher reassured him that he needn't worry about his grades. She explained that if he concentrated on his music, colleges would excuse his average grades in light of his musical talent. Kurt's average grades became poor. He used his teacher's comment as an excuse for not completing homework assignments.

Here's what you could do if your children were in a similar situation, whether it be a music teacher, sports coach or drama director.

1. Contact the teacher or coach and ask for a private conference without your child's presence.

2. Indicate to the teacher or coach how much you appreciate the inspirational model that he/she has provided for your child.

3. Explain that your child is misinterpreting part of what he/she is saying and has used that to avoid school responsibility.

4. Point out to the teacher that he or she is very important in your child's life and that you want to encourage this positive relationship.

5. Ask the teacher to rephrase the message so that your child may better prepare for alternative careers. Explain to the teacher your concern about leaving other avenues open should your child not be successful in these highly competitive fields.

6. Be assured. The teacher will understand and probably had no intention of giving the message your child chose to hear.

Family Members. Sometimes role models are grandparents, aunts, uncles or relatives who care and love your child but are unintentionally giving inappropriate learning messages. This may be very difficult for you since these important others may be sabotaging your messages about the importance of school learning. Here's a case example of grandparent sabotage:

Terrance was an only child and the first and only grandchild. Terrance's parents came into the Clinic because they found his behavior impossible to control at home. His mother, working full time, found herself avoiding coming home because her son was so difficult. Father's attitude wasn't much better. I was able to give the parents some simple control techniques (see Chapter 1) which effectively set Terrance's limits, but wasn't surprised to find out that a major component of Terrance's overpowering behavior was caused by grandparent sabotage. For example, if Mother was disappointed at Terrance's poor behavior at school, Grandmother's response would be, "Well he can't be perfect. He's just a little boy. You weren't so perfect at school either."

If you have a relative who is providing an inappropriate role model or negating your good modeling, try the following:

1. Tell your relative in a firm, loving way that you value them as role models for your children.

2. Explain that your children are also hearing negative messages and ask them to change those specific communications.

3. If the messages are very negative and if the important adults ignore your request, you'll want to take a firmer stand. Tell them that if they continue, you'll prevent your children from seeing them. Remind them that you don't want to do that, but their actions must stop. Be firm, but be loving and caring to those people who love your children so much. It would be sad to cut these relationships and much better if you can improve the role models that these important relatives are to your children.

OLD BATTLE RENEWED

GRANDMA, I GOT IN TROUBLE AT SCHOOL. I'M AFRAID TO TELL MOM.

DON'T WORRY, RANDY. YOUR MOM WASN'T SO GOOD EITHER. I'LL REMIND HER.

After Divorce. If the role model is the child's other birth parent whom you wish the child would not have to even know, point out the good qualities of that person and de-emphasize the negative qualities. Don't discuss your frustration at the other person's power in your life. Powerful people are more likely to be selected as role models. For example, constant reminders to the children of your dependence on financial support maintains your former spouse's power and makes you appear powerless. Never remind your children of how similar they are to your former spouse in either negative or positive ways. Instead, point out similarities of your children to other important relatives who you see as potentially positive role models. Tell your son he reminds you of your own dad or your daughter of your mother. Tell either they remind you of yourself — or at least of your positive characteristics.

Literature and Television Heroes. If your children have chosen good role models from books or television, point out the similarities between your children and those role models. Provide a more in-depth picture of those role models. For example, children often assume that television role models like rock stars or professional football players have had effortless success. You may want to point out their tremendous amounts of required practice and effort. In that way, the child can learn to work and make real effort in a chosen direction. You might also point to others in these particular career fields, who despite tremendous efforts, have not been successful and have had to select other options. In this way, you'll be preparing your children not only for effort and hard work, but for the importance of selecting alternatives should they change their first career choice or not qualify. Don't emphasize their lucky breaks or you may find your children sitting around, doing nothing and waiting for their "lucky breaks."

Placing Yourself and/or Your Spouse Back on a Pedestal. Be assertive in designing yourself or your spouse as appropriate role models. Parents have become hesitant about using their own power as role models for their children. They prefer to tell their children that they don't want to choose for them. They want their children to find their own way and their own career and children often accept that as a message **not** to choose a parent's career. They even feel that it is a negative statement about their independence should they select a similar career to one of their parents.

What's wrong with children following in their parents' footsteps? Has that become "un-American?" In efforts not to limit their children's options and independence, parents often resign as potential role models for their own children. This leaves a role-model vacuum. Adolescents spontaneously search out role models in an effort to establish their identity. If parents refuse to inspire their children as role models, the children must seek others and may choose them by chance. Parents should make a deliberate effort either to establish themselves as potential role models or to guide their children toward situations where they will have contact with a circle of appropriate role models from which to choose. Mentors, teachers, business acquaintances or your friends may provide excellent optional role models. Don't disqualify yourselves, particularly if you have interesting careers.

Peer Role Models. During adolescence it's normal to view peers as at least partial role models. If parents have resigned from modeling by not building alliances or appropriate identification with their children, if adolescents have become completely oppositional and if they're not exposed to other appropriate role models, peers may become their only role models. That may

218

219

or may not be positive depending on the peer group that surrounds your adolescents. If popularity or adjustment to peers has been a value emphasized to your children, then it's even more likely that their peer group will take priority as role models. In our society today, "popular" students are not necessarily safe friends or competent role models (see Popularity Ends at Grade Twelve, Rimm, 1988). Thus, it becomes very important to communicate early about peer independence. By adolescence, they will have internalized much of your early advice. If you teach a priority of "adjustment" to friends, it may backfire by your children's preteen years.

Here are some messages that parents and teachers often give children when they're in elementary school which may cause them problems later.

Case 1

Bobby is working alone on an independent science project or reading a book. It's recess and his teacher reminds him to go out to play because all the other children are on the playground. Bobby asks permission to stay in, saying, "I'd like to finish my project if I may." The teacher thinks Bobby is a "loner" and insists, "No, it's time for play. You should be with the other kids." He interrupts his intrinsically rewarding, independent learning experience to go out and join the other kids at play. The teacher believes she is teaching socially appropriate behavior and good adjustment.

Case 2

On the weekend, Scott chooses to play at home with the family. You're concerned about his friendship adjustment and say to him, "Scott, you haven't had a friend over since last week. Don't you think it would be good to have a friend over?" Your son's response is, "I had a friend over last week so I thought this week I'd be with the family, but if you want me to, I'll call my friend." Based on Mom's or Dad's suggestion he invites a friend over. He's been given a message about how important it is to have a friend over on the weekend for good adjustment.

Case 3

Debbie comes home from school and says to you, "Mom (or Dad), Marlene didn't invite me to her birthday party. She invited eight girls and didn't invite six and I was in the group that wasn't invited. Marlene is my friend and I feel very sad."

You, in an attempt to help Debbie with her social adjustment, say, "Well, I'm sorry you weren't invited to Marlene's party. Do you suppose there's something that you did wrong that caused Marlene not to include you in her group of friends? I know you like her."

And Debbie responds, "Well, the last time Marlene wanted me to play kicker, I preferred playing on the swing set with the other kids. Do you suppose that might be the reason that she didn't invite me?"

And Mom or Dad say, "Well, Debbie, that's probably the reason. You'll want to be more willing to do what Marlene wants you to, if you want to be invited to her party." Debbie heard your message and has internalized that as good adjustment.

When these children reach junior high or middle school, where there seems to be the greatest amount of peer pressure, they act on those internalized values and repeat them to parents and teachers. However, neither parents nor teachers recognize the origin of the message nor are they happy about the effects.

Teachers ask me, "Why is it that our middle school youngsters are not willing to work independently or learn for the sake of learning?" When Bobby doesn't work by himself, they say to him, "Bobby, why aren't you able to follow through on a project." Bobby's response is, "But I'd rather be outside playing with my friends. This project is boring."

When Scott is busy all weekend with his peers or friends and can't find time to do anything with the family, Mom or Dad ask, "Scott, why don't you make time to be with the family?"

They hear from Scott, "I'd rather be with my friends. Family stuff is boring."

When Debbie comes home from Marlene's party and her mother can smell the alcohol on her breath and she questions Debbie, in distress, "How could you do something that you know is illegal and is against all the health values that we've taught you?"

Debbie looks up at Mother with a tear rolling down her cheek and says, "But Mom, Marlene wouldn't invite me to the party if I didn't go along with the rest of the kids."

The advice that you give during childhood for good social adjustment is often internalized as standards by which adolescents will abide. In the name of friendship, they have been taught to identify with, feel close to and value their peers as their only mentors and models. The message that you should give your children most frequently and most diligently is to be independent, to do their own work, to develop interests, to enjoy their family and to be able to say "no" despite peer pressure. Otherwise, the emphasis on popularity,

an antinerd, antigeek, antilearning standard will begin influencing your children by grade five and usually continue through grade eleven. It interferes with your children's love of learning and their adoption of positive adult role models.

We can only fight that empty value system by teaching our children that popularity is temporary and disappears as an important value right after their senior year in high school. In college and in careers, although people continue to value leadership, sociability and friendship, the concept of popularity disappears. Popularity is only a competitive form of friendship. Having the most friends with the most parties is not an essential element in most careers, in successful marriages or in creative and happy lives.

As parents, you'll find that the popularity message is a difficult one to combat. We often counteridentify with our children's valuing of their popularity and we too see it as a symbol of their success. I ask you to overtly devalue popularity to your children. Instead, value the qualities of good friendship including shared interests, support, kindness and wholesome fun. Reasonably similar values should be a number one priority recommended for friendship or you'll find your children being controlled by peer groups who represent antilearning, antischool and antiparent norms. You obviously shouldn't select all your children's friends but do give them a basis for friendship selection. Friends will influence your children's progress toward self-confidence and accomplishment.

Setting Expectations

My mother expects me to get all As.

My parents put so much pressure on me.

224

I'll never be able to satisfy my father.

My parents expect me to be as smart as my sister.

They expect me to be perfect.

All my parents want me to do is work, work, work.

This sample of descriptions about parents' expectations is typical of those voiced by many of the children who visit our Clinic. Most are difficult to trace, although the last one, about work, came from a 16-year-old who was required to do the family dishes nightly (and a very small family at that). Parents can rarely understand how their children have such mistaken understandings of their expectations. It takes some therapist detective work to uncover the relationship between what parents are saying and what children are perceiving. The discrepancy between the two emphasizes the importance of clarification of expectations by parents.

Expectations should be clarified relative to moral values, social behaviors, home responsibilities and schoolwork. Frequently, the assumption is made that children know what's expected and that there is no need for explicit information. On the other hand, some parents talk so much about expectations that there is continuous family argument and debate. Sometimes so little is expected that a parent request feels monumental compared to what children usually accomplish. Either too much or too little may cause parents and children misunderstandings.

If you don't set explicit expectations for your children, they will assume that those behaviors which you praise represent your expectations and that those

behaviors which you condemn or punish, are those that disappoint you. Your praise and condemnation of others' behaviors are also incorporated into their perspectives of your expectations. Here's an example:

Alison often refused to go to school. Even when she attended, she might skip classes and sit in the library reading. When she discussed her feelings about school with me, she pointed out that she was disappointed in herself and felt sure that her mom and dad were disappointed in her as well. She indicated that she thought that her mom expected her to get all As.

In discussion with her mother about realistic expectations, she responded that she would be delighted if Alison got Bs and Cs. She wanted mainly for Alison to attend class and get her schoolwork done.

In our next session, I again discussed with Alison her perception of her mother's expectations. Alison's question to me was, "Why else would my mother say, 'If you would only do your work, you would surely get As.'?" Her mother's attempts to build Alison's confidence were interpreted as expectations.

Alison's older brother was mainly an A student and so she had observed the praise that he was given for his excellent grade point average. She further assumed that there were similar expectations for her. Despite my clarification of her mother's expectations, Alison was not convinced. Alison had already internalized a set of personal expectations for As and was blaming those on her mom.

Children also become confused and may believe that expectations they have of themselves are the expectations their parents have of them. Thus, when they're disappointed in their own performance, they may say that they haven't lived up to what their parents expected of them. Sometimes they blame one parent more than the other and bring their complaints to the other. For example, "I can never satisfy Dad" may become a request for Mother's easy way out.

Mom, here's your counter. "I know Dad expects a lot of you. You wouldn't want him not to. If he didn't, it would mean he thinks you're not that smart. Just the other day, he was mentioning to me how pleased he is with your hard work."

That will send your daughter or son back to the workplace with new confidence and no easy way out.

And for you, Dad, when you hear, "Mom expects all *A*s." "Mom does set high standards for you. She knows you're really smart. She was just telling me how pleased she was that you were able to bring your *C* in Honors Math to a *B*. It puts a little pressure on all of us to do hard things well. Keep up the good work!"

Notice that these statements: 1) diffuse the battle, 2) build an alliance for children with you and your spouse, 3) give a message of confidence to your children and 4) clarify expectations. If you really do feel concerned about too high expectations that your spouse may have set, after you've accomplished these diffusion/alliance/confidence/clarification conversations, do talk to your spouse about your concerns (review Chapter 2 if this is an area where you should have more practice).

You can see that expectations can become quite complex if they aren't specifically stated. It's critical that your expectations be realistic in terms of your

children's abilities and that the expectations are established in ways that enable children to follow through effectively.

Expectations in basic areas of life should be stated clearly, briefly and simply to children. They should understand exactly what their parents' value system is, which values they are expected to follow through on and where they can make their own choices. You don't want to give children a hundred rules. The more rules you give, the less they assume you trust them. Stay positive and simple.

Once you've stated your expectations clearly, follow through to be sure children complete their home and school responsibilities. When they don't meet your expectations, avoid getting into an arguing mode with them. Simply state that you're disappointed about their lying or dishonesty or poor effort in school. Indicate what you expect in the future and what negative consequences will follow if they don't meet your reasonable standards. Stay in a positive alliance with your child but follow through with promised punishments if necessary. A note of caution. Don't state your expectations in front of their adolescent peers. That's an invitation to opposition if their peers are oppositional.

Schoolwork is Central. The most important expectation relative to school achievement is that academic learning is central while all other school-related activities are of lesser importance or peripheral. Thus band, chorus, sports and drama are important in that they provide a full and enriched life for children and adults alike. Certainly, developing interests and involvement in competitive activities in those areas is appropriate and should be encouraged, but schoolwork and study should have first priority. If that message is clearly stated when children are younger, they will

know by high school that geometry homework is to be completed even though play rehearsals last until 9:30, and that a heavy basketball schedule is not an excuse for skipping a class because homework isn't done.

Actually, there are many parents who inadvertently send the opposite message. For example, one parent informed me that she told her gifted, academically un-challenged daughter that the most important part of school was her extracurricular activities. She unintention-ally gave a clear message to her child to underachieve.

Parents who take children out of school for shopping trips and sports events are sending messages about the unimportance of schoolwork. When children are excused from school, there should be an educational or medical reason for that excuse. Field trips or family trips which provide unique learning experiences ob-viously qualify. If other family events should make it necessary for you to take your children out of school, then emphasize school importance by requiring your children to collect and complete all school assign-ments, preferably beforehand. This will provide reasonable flexibility for you while continuing to com-municate your valuing of academic responsibility.

The central versus peripheral message is especially important to children because their special area of talent, expertise or showmanship, feels so much more enticing than the more mundane activities of the classroom. If your children demonstrate unusual com-petence in a talent area, you could ask the school to make allowances for their special training or practice needs. It may be that such gifted children should have a lightened number of academic requirements. How-ever, they should be cautioned to maintain at least the minimum number to permit them to select alternate

career options. Good quality standards should be expected for all subjects. It's difficult to know which may be important for alternative careers. For example, the aspiring dramatic actress eventually may be forced to compromise and teach drama and English. Although that may seem an unlikely outcome for the star of the high school production of *Carousel* or *Fiddler on the Roof*, he or she certainly will have to learn math and science to continue for that college degree.

Many youths, from first grade through college, have declared to me their rationalizations for not studying or doing homework in subjects they are certain are irrelevant to their future. "Why do I need science if I'm going to become a famous rock star?" I've become convinced that some parents are inferring to their children that teachers don't know anything about good education. Of course, this may likely also represent selective listening on the part of their children. There truly is a basic core of skills that educated citizens should master by adulthood. Parents should communicate to their children that they're expected to learn to read, write and do math even if they "hate" all of those subjects and are grooming themselves for professional football or the ballet.

These suggestions should never be interpreted as nonsupport for music, art, drama or athletics. To the contrary, all of these forms of creative enrichment are extremely important. However, for most children they should be viewed as supplementary to the core of good academic learning and thinking.

Perfectionism and Competition. Judging by the children who come to our Clinic, the related issues of perfectionism and competition are high on their list of problems. Although so many children and adolescents are affected by these pressures, only rarely do the children, their parents or their teachers recognize these underlying causes of their problems. Here are some case examples:

Case 1

Glen is a bright, third-grade, little boy who is having behavior problems in school. He's not an aggressive kid but he talks out, monopolizes class conversation, walks around the classroom and does attention-getting acting out. In his gifted class, which meets an hour a week, he's very quiet, subdued and hardly ever volunteers.

Case 2

Marie, an eighth grader is going to a party. She looks at herself in the mirror and says, "Gee, I look really nice." She gets to the party, looks at everyone else and says, "I'm just not pretty enough, I'm just not thin enough, I look terrible."

Case 3

Peter, an eighth grader, is very, very oppositional at home, disrespectful to both his mom and dad. He was underachieving at school and teased by other kids. We helped him reverse his underachievement pattern in one quarter of a school year. His "perfect" sister writes a letter to her parents. "Dear Mom and Dad, I'm not going to work in school anymore because you just care about my brother and not me."

Case 4

A college student drops out of college in the first semester of his freshman year even though he has had a 3.6 average in high school. The only symptom that suggested the parenting problem was his high school basketball activities. When he wasn't first-string on the basketball team, he quit.

Case 5

Ron, a college student found himself feeling depressed whenever he didn't earn an *A*. He wasn't able to understand the reason for his depressed feelings.

What do all of these youths have in common? They are all having trouble coping with competition. All of them want to be number one and the best and when that doesn't happen, they either quit, are depressed or act out in some other way.

Competition is pervasive in our society. That means that there is competition in families, competition in classrooms and competition among friends. Yet we typically think of competition in only the sports world. Let's backtrack and spotlight the competition problem for each of these young people.

For the third-grade boy, his competitive stresses were directed toward being the smartest child in the class. In his regular classroom he tried to demonstrate this by bragging and trying to complete his work first. He would speak out of turn and talk as long as possible. In the more competitive gifted classroom, he felt like a loser in competition and was afraid to take the risk of contributing his ideas. He became very quiet.

The eighth-grade girl looked at herself and thought she looked nice until she went to the party. Then she compared herself to everyone else and decided she wasn't as pretty or as thin as everyone else.

For the oppositional boy who had a "perfect sister," I had warned his parents that his change would impact on his sister. They said, "It won't. She's practically perfect. She gets all As, she's responsible, she's just a good kid." When her brother reversed his problems and became "a good kid," she felt dethroned. She didn't understand why she was no longer number one in the family. She started acting out. That happens all the time. I always prepare parents for sibling competitive effects.

For the college student dropout, the tip-off showed in basketball where he had been a star until he was taken off the first-string team. He was an academic star as well. As soon as he wasn't a star, he quit basketball. When he went to college, the competition was keen. He couldn't be a star — he quit there too.

The college boy, who was depressed by his Bs, was one of the top students in his high school class — a very, very bright student. He described himself as not feeling as if he was a competitive person. When he got a B and realized that some other students were getting As, he didn't recognize that his depression was caused by losing in competition.

Competition does affect all of us and, as parents, you will want to model and set expectations for coping with it.

We usually think about competition for children as it relates to sports or games. Actually competition generalizes to every area of your children's lives. There may be competition at home between siblings, or with one parent or the other. There may be competition

between cousins or close friends. The classroom is a competitive arena where teachers and children make competitive comparisons frequently.

Children respond to competition directly, intellectually, as well as in apparently unrelated areas which impact greatly on achievement and intellectual growth. Children compete obviously in specific skills such as art, music or sports. They compete also to be most socially successful (popularity), most creative (different), most oppositional (rebellious), most muscular, most beautiful and thinnest. All of these competitive pressures contribute to their self-image which may include or exclude the image of being intelligent. Some highly competitive children will choose an area where they see themselves as expert and use that excellence as an excuse for not performing in academic work, where they may not see themselves as successful.

Teaching children to live in a competitive society means guiding them toward handling both winning and losing, succeeding and failing. Children who have mainly had failure experiences, avoid competition for fear of further failures. Schools without failure and curriculum that provide only successes don't provide children with risk-taking experiences. Children who succeed all the time or who get all *A*s effortlessly are not prepared for a competitive society. They've learned to function only in a world without challenge. Their self-confidence is dependent on being first, perfect, at the top and always winning. When they find themselves in situations where they're somewhat less successful, second best or surrounded by other extremely intelligent people, they may feel like failures. Their confidence falters dramatically and they may feel defeated or depressed. If they've learned to function in competition, they reset their goals, view their failure as a temporary setback and persevere whether in the same direction or in an appropriate substitute direction.

In teaching your children to function in competition, first examine your own competitive style; children may have learned maladaptive responses to failure from you. For example, you may model an attitude of quitting too quickly if a problem gets difficult, of avoiding all competition or of habitually blaming others for your own shortcomings or lack of effort. You may even be a perfectionist.

Children should be taught to identify creative alternatives for their losses or failures. For example, they should recognize that normal people, even very talented ones, can't be "Number One" in everything (or anything permanently) but that every person has areas in which they're talented. They shouldn't feel insecure or threatened by an occasional setback. Your discussion of your child's failure may need to wait until after the emotional tension is reduced in order to avoid their defensive behaviors. Parents can't expect rational perception of logical thinking during the immediate stress period following an upsetting defeat.

A questioning approach, rather than lecture, may better help your children understand that 1) they can't always win, 2) their losses don't mean they're failures, 3) the particular experience simply wasn't as successful as they'd hoped it would be, 4) everyone would like to be smarter than they are, and especially, 5) the main goal is to play the learning game at their best performance level, regardless of their competitive ranking. Effort counts. And humor helps.

Comparing school to sports is a wonderful way for children to learn about being a good team member, striving for their personal best, "being a good sport,"

not hogging the spotlight or hurting the team by their heroics, congratulating the winner and coping with "striking out." Parents who share sports involvement with children can help make the relevant comparisons to schoolwork. The same rules apply.

Teaching admiration, as a strategy for handling jealousy, is another means of developing sensitivity which can assist your children in the real world. Even while your children are winning, they can learn to notice, admire and communicate their admiration to other performers. Since they're in the habit of competing, other persons' victories make them feel inadequate by comparison. When they meet real competition, even when it's on the other team, the gracious "good sport" should develop skill at admiring and respecting, rather than deprecating the talent of their rivals. Although it's truly a difficult skill for highly competitive children to develop, it gives them a mentally healthy way to deal with being second best. If you stress that winning, regardless of the game, is so important, then winning at tennis, on the swim team or in popularity contests may become too crucial to your children.

Even as you enthusiastically share your children's victories and commiserate with their defeats, remind them (and yourself) that "regardless of performance, there's always someone better than them and there's always someone worse."* Explain to your children that there is no such place as Number One. First place is only temporary. If they're first on one level, they'll soon be competing on a higher level with other persons who were also first. Although it's fun to keep competing and trying, it's not reasonable to expect to stay in first place.

---

*This may sound like a famous quotation but as far as I can tell, this bit of philosophy which guided our children through competition was stated mainly (and frequently) by their dad, Alfred Rimm.

That concept holds true if their talent area is sports, music, art, math, science, debate or any other. It's probably better for them to learn to set reasonable goals, one step at a time, than dream of stardom before they've discovered all their own talents and the discipline necessary for success.

You shouldn't really pin your parent identity hopes on your children becoming tennis champs, Olympic swimmers, Picassos or Beethovens. The arts and sports fields are overcrowded and extraordinarily competitive. Certainly encourage their talents, but don't permit them to bypass studies or academic requirements or you may find yourself supporting your talented artists for life.

Explain to your children that they should make family and friendship as noncompetitive as possible. They may feel and express jealous feelings, but they should continue to try to build support, encouragement and admiration into these relationships. You can teach them to "feel neat about having a whole smart family" or to think it feels good to have a friend who is so successful. You can help them to feel caring and sensitive when a sibling or friend does less well than they and to express understanding and support to these friends. These are difficult feelings for children to work through.

In order to develop a skill where children lack confidence, they should learn to compete with their own past performance instead of with others. For example, if they're having problems with timed math tests at school, they may take the same test daily at home, timing themselves each time and charting their time. Their daily goal should be to beat yesterday's time. They may soon find that they have exceeded teacher expectations by beating their own record. This works well with tasks of endurance as well as speed.

Sometimes you may find your children "shutting down" in an area where they're fairly talented. You may wonder why your child who wins an art contest stops painting or your child whose writing or music you admired no longer writes or plays. Children don't understand why they shut down so don't expect them to explain it. They're responding to perfectionism and competition. Here's a story from my own childhood which may help you to understand. You may have had similar experiences.

I always loved to write. The first books, stories and poems that I can remember writing were when I was in fourth grade. Perhaps there were some even earlier. In sixth grade, I wrote a creative composition about how I had gotten lost in New York City. My teacher thought it was wonderful and I considered it the best I had ever written. Suddenly I found myself stuck. Every assignment that year brought me back to the same topic. I explained to my teacher that I just couldn't think of anything more to write about. I truly couldn't. I was sure I couldn't find a topic as good as my last story. For the remainder of that school year, I hated and avoided all writing assignments. The next school year was better although I continued to feel inadequate until eighth grade when I wrote a marvelous imaginative piece on how it felt to be a slave during the Civil War. I can still remember my feelings as my class sat spellbound listening to my A+ story. That excellence almost stopped me again. As a result of my slavery story, I was chosen to write a competitive essay for a graduation contest. I tried to use a creative approach for the contest comparing Washington D.C. as the heart of our nation, to the heart of a person. My teacher considered it to be an inappropriate style for the contest. I was confused. I botched something together which my teacher thought was poor. That stifled my creative writing throughout high school. I was asked to work on the high school yearbook and had so little confidence that I volunteered to be the typist.

It took years to renew my courage. There may be a few of you readers who may feel that it would have been better had I not returned to writing. That would hurt my feelings, but no one could stop me now. I love to write and I have received enough positive feedback from readers to know that my straightforward conversational writing style reaches them. I enjoy writing so much that airplanes, airports and even vacations are improved if I have my pen in hand.

I hope that my sharing with you my own struggle with competition and perfectionism permits you some further insight on how your children feel when faced with the fear that they may not be winners by comparison to their own past performance. You can see that reminding them of their own past excellence will only increase their feelings of pressure. Teaching them about personal brainstorming (see Chapter 3) and encouraging fooling around with artistic ideas gives children permission to produce without always winning.

Boredom. Teaching children to cope with competition may feel like a "piece of cake" compared to interpreting to children the usefulness of boredom. Boredom appears to be the major complaint of most American children who don't like school or a particular class. Parents and teachers sometimes miss the fact that boring may mean different things to different kids. Interpreting what boring means for your children provides a special challenge. You'll only be able to help them if you know what their "boring" means and they may not be sure of how to interpret their own boredom. (Remember Chapter 1, How Do children Think, as you read this section.)

Boring may mean lack of challenge or too much challenge. It may mean sitting still too long or too little activity. It may include too much written work or too much reading. For some children, boring means schoolwork lacks action or humor or a creative outlet. Sometimes children who must sacrifice chatting with their friends consider school to be boring. Boring or irrelevant may be used to describe high school work that adolescents don't see as applying to their own immediate lives or goals (and they seem to believe that they know exactly what those are). However, the most frequent use of boring generally refers to children's inner fears that they will not be able to accomplish the work well enough to be considered very smart. Thus, it serves as a defense and an excuse for avoidance of effort (back to perfectionism and competition).

If your children's abilities and skills and the curriculum are mismatched, either too easy or too hard, don't hesitate to arrange a conference with their teacher. The "too hard" is relatively easy to communicate; the "too easy" is almost always more difficult to share with teachers. Bring samples of work your children have accomplished independently at home to demonstrate their skills and interests. Don't assume that the teachers aren't challenging your children. Be positive. Don't blame the teachers. Share with the teachers the concerns you've heard voiced by your children. Listen to their view of your children's skills. If the teachers don't convince you that your children are challenged, recommend experimenting with end

BORING! WHAT DOES IT MEAN?
TOO HARD!
TOO MUCH TO WRITE.
TOO EASY.
"SCHOOL IS BORING!"
I DON'T KNOW WHAT TO DO!
NOT ENOUGH ACTION
TOO MUCH WORK!

of chapter or book testing to determine what they already know. Hopefully, the teacher will be willing to individualize, or even better, place your children in appropriately challenging groups.

Many teachers complain because gifted children perform poor quality work in the name of their boredom. A nice technique which pleases most is shortening the next assignment based on excellence. For example, if math assignment number one is excellent, they're only required to do three-fourths or half of math assignment number two. If that's excellent, shortened assignments continue. If quality drops, quantity increases. Gifted children are usually delighted to be reinforced by less repetitive work and are willing to emphasize quality "to get out of" what they may term "busywork." This solution usually pleases their teachers as well.

If the problem doesn't improve, you may wish to discuss your concerns with the teacher of the gifted in your school or with the principal. Be sure not to blame the problem on the teacher, but do ask for assistance.

As you try to determine your children's appropriate academic placement, caution your children to continue to do their best work despite their boredom. Don't permit them to use boredom as an excuse for avoiding work.

If your children complain that their boring work is easy, remind them that they are expected to challenge themselves. Going beyond assignments and searching for extra work is an appropriate responsibility for gifted children. They can share their products with their parents or with their class. Encourage your children to become involved in independent projects which reflect and extend their interest. This is an area where you, as parents, can also become involved. You can either explore an interest with them, facilitate opportunities for them or provide feedback and encouragement for their work. If they can tie their individual work into a school subject or presentation, so much the better. If not, you, your spouse and their siblings or grandparents may be the only audience for their efforts. They do like feedback. Don't expect them to keep themselves busy on individual projects if you and their teachers are uninterested.

Your children's pursuit of knowledge can be fostered by praise statements that prize curiosity, follow-through, perseverance, interest and quality. Model intrinsic interest by being interested and interesting in your own leisure pursuits.

When children are assigned ambiguous tasks like writing a story or report or doing a science project, they may describe these as boring if they're having problems getting started. Don't get into the habit of providing them with multiple-choice suggestions. That's easy to do, but doesn't provide them techniques for the future. You produce an idea and they say that isn't any good. Of course, they use the same pattern when they try to produce their own ideas. Instead, teach children how to brainstorm for their own ideas (Davis & Rimm, 1989, 1985; Rimm, 1986). When they become accustomed to divergent-thinking techniques, they'll be less likely to label open-ended assignments as boring.

Long-term projects may also be labeled as boring if children feel overwhelmed by the size of the assigned project. Teachers often break these down into subparts and that may certainly help. If that hasn't been done by the school, it's a skill you can teach to your children at home. You may show them what you do when you feel overwhelmed with your own work, for example, making lists and setting time lines. Encourage them to check with you as they complete their step-by-step tasks.

Involving children in adult-child partnerships or boring tasks is perhaps the best way to model persevering through boredom. Humor is a critical ingredient in moving through tasks that are necessary but boring. One of our sons' favorite humorous memories is of tarring the inside of the silo so that it would hold water for irrigating our orchard. I believe they attempted that task several times — always unsuccessfully. The boys learned a great deal of perseverance in a boring task which they made into a ridiculous task. (It was a ridiculous task that never worked for the orchard, but did for them.)

Here are some case examples of children's experiences with boredom. All improved after appropriate interpretation of boredom.

Case 1

Steve, a 16-year-old sophomore with slightly above-average ability, had done no homework since fifth grade. When I asked him how he liked school, he said he enjoyed it. Furthermore, he explained that he enjoyed learning and loved discussions. He actually considered himself to be an "intellectual." I told him that there seemed to be a mismatch between his love of learning and his refusal to do homework. He justified his refusal by indicating that homework was "boring" and that he absolutely could not do boring work.

The increasing number of Fs on his report card made it appear likely that Steve might not be graduating from high school. Without a high school diploma, Steve might well be doomed to doing boring work as a lifetime career. I pointed out that for an intelligent young man, factory assembly line work, if he could qualify for that, might feel exactly like prison. For just a moment this "tough" young man's eyes seemed to gloss over betraying the sadness and anxiety he was not willing to express verbally. I knew that not doing his homework had become part of a power struggle he wasn't willing to acknowledge losing and that the struggle was part of his worry about not being as intelligent as he wanted to appear. Not doing his schoolwork was also a rather strong family tradition. His father, an acknowledged underachiever, was still providing a battery of excuses for both himself and his son.

Case 2

Bob, an intellectually gifted seventh grader, had been underachieving since he entered school. Furthermore, he argued with both his parents and physically abused his mother. He literally pushed her around when he could not convince her to permit him to do as he wished. With help from our Clinic, his parents and teachers worked together and Bob made rapid strides in his achievement. His parents learned quickly how to handle his power struggles and all seemed to be going much better at home and at school.

Bob's mother questioned one major power struggle which didn't seem to make sense to her. Bob had been given a poetry assignment by his teacher in his enrichment class. He briefly regressed to his early procrastination problem and didn't do his poetry assignment until the very last minute. As he put off doing his work, he protested continually to his mom about the "boring" poetry assignment. His mother, not hearing the real message, tried rationally to argue the merits of writing poetry. She found herself becoming more impatient.

When Bob finally completed his poem, he received very positive feedback from his teacher. The poetry flowed thereafter and lost its reputation for boredom. "Boring" was the word Bob used for "afraid I will not be able to be gifted in this new form of expression." The earlier pattern of fear of risk taking restored itself when Bob was faced with this ambiguous poetry assignment and mother, attending to his words instead of his immense fears, found herself back in the argument trap.

Case 3

Skipper was a seven-year-old first grader. I asked him how he liked school. His response was that school was a "humdrum world." He said he preferred Mousey Town, the pretend world of his nine imaginary playmates. Skipper scored 147+ on his WISC-R IQ test. His reading tested at seventh grade, eighth month, and his math at a fourth-grade level. His first-grade teacher said he was immature and that he would certainly adjust by third grade. He didn't read with a reading group but was permitted to do reading alone at a slightly more advanced level. He did math with the class. The kids thought he was "weird."

Skipper's humdrum world was a combination or lack of intellectual challenge and peer relationship problems. He knew he was very bright and was even anxious to make an effort and persevere. However, there was no place for him to fit in, either academically or socially. Boring meant lack of challenge and loneliness for Skipper.

Setting Grade Expectations

Parents that I meet with at our Clinic are usually pretty reasonable in setting grade expectations for their children. However, most parents are unsure of whether or not they are being reasonable. They've been told so frequently that parents expect too much of their children that they tend to be somewhat defensive and fear that maybe they're expecting too much.

In general, a rule-of-thumb guideline that you might want to use in thinking about reasonable grade expectations follows: Children who are in the gifted range of abilities can be expected to get an *A/B* average. More *A*s than *B*s are appropriate, but it's unreasonable to expect a perfect grade point of your children. Obviously, if they do get a perfect *A* grade point one quarter, parents can feel proud and good about it. If that's their consistent pattern, it certainly gives children a sense of pride. However, setting it as an expectation puts a great deal of pressure on them.

Schools that use a 4.0 or perfect grade point as the basis for their high honor roll are, in fact, not only causing a few children a great deal of pressure, but are causing other children who are excellent students to feel as if they can't ever work to the level of high honor roll. A high honor roll that requires a 3.7 or a 3.8 average certainly documents excellent student performance without putting perfectionistic pressures on very bright children.

Children who have above-average ability, should be expected to be able to earn a *B* average. There may be some *A*s, an occasional *C*, but a *B* to *B+* average for such children is a reasonable goal. Children with average ability can be expected to get a *B-* or *C+* average. *B*s or *C*s could be their typical grades. An occasional *A* in an area of strength or an occasional

D in a very difficult subject also are reasonable grades. Children who have somewhat below-average abilities can expect to obtain a *C* average with an occasional *D* or an occasional *B*. For the most part, teachers don't give *D*s to children who are responsible, get all their homework in, show a positive attitude about learning and are in attendance regularly.

The grade ranges described are based on typical schools. There is variation from elementary to high school with slightly higher grade point averages expected at elementary school and slighter lower grade point averages in highly academic high schools.

Course selection may also affect grade expectation. Highly academic and honors courses may demand more of children. If the school weights these honors courses, for example (gives 5.0 for an *A*, 4.0 for a *B*, etc.), then you may need to adjust your expectations. The school may be able to provide you with further insight about reasonable goals for your children under special circumstances.

Variations for private schools should be considered since independent schools have a reputation for using a lower/harder grading system than public schools. Usually their scales compared to most public schools, would be one grade lower.

Any generalization you make about grading will have its exceptions and you, as parents, should get some sense of what school expectations and grading systems represent. The best and fairest way to set your children's expectations is by observing their efforts. If they're conscientious, if they get all their homework in, if they prepare for tests and invest time in concentrated study, then the grade outcomes are likely to be a good and fair fit with their abilities. Observe those efforts and give your children a sense of expectations

based on efforts. You can be reasonably sure that your expectations fit with their abilities if they are hard workers. Study guidelines, that you structure for your children, should be based on efforts and responsibilities (see Chapter 2). You may, of course, wish to have regular feedback from teachers if your children's direct feedack is not dependable. However, for children who are already achievers, regular teacher conference feedback is usually sufficient.

Setting Post-High School Expectations

Children, from early on, can be given a sense of what parents expect of in terms of long-term academic goals. Obviously, parents should be sufficiently flexible to allow young adults make final decisions. Setting reasonably high academic expectations will make it much more likely that your children will accept the challenge of higher education. Again, those expectations can be based on early indications of your children's abilities.

Children who are in the gifted range may be expected to achieve beyond a college bachelor's degree. A master's or doctorate degree may be set as reasonable, depending on their career choice and the degree requirements of that career. For children in the above-average range of ability, expectations for a four-year college or technical program are certainly appropriate. For children within average ranges or somewhat below-average abilities, parents should expect completion of high school as well as completion of some kind of technical or post-high school training whether it be junior or technical college or a career training program. In our society today and tomorrow, youth who have educated themselves for careers which will provide work satisfaction and a reasonable wage, are going to be happier. There's nothing wrong with parents setting higher education as a reasonable expectation. If parents don't state their expectations, children don't guess them and don't internalize any goal direction. They'll only be influenced by their peer group or other adults. Thus, while parents shouldn't be rigid in setting expectations, they should certainly set a range and assume that children will educate themselves within that range. That should not cause capable children feelings of undue pressure but should, instead, encourage their motivation toward learning.

Grading and post-high school education guidelines should only be considered **guidelines**. Don't make the mistake of not expecting your child to do well because of IQ test scores which you may perceive as a permanent limitation for your children. IQ scores are not engraved in stone and there is no way to truly measure intelligence. An IQ score may, by chance, be lower than what the child is capable of producing in school. IQ scores may also have decreased over time because the child has been underachieving.

Certainly I have seen many children whose IQ scores were in the average range who were able to achieve *A*s and *B*s throughout high school, though they rarely were able to attain those high grades in advanced mathematics or advanced science courses. Again, IQ tests don't measure all kinds of abilities, only some kinds.

Before you make yourself feel guilty for expecting your children to perform better than teachers are saying you should expect, observe the process. Remember that if your children are working, doing their homework and being responsible, don't expect them to get higher grades than what they're getting. They may be able to benefit from learning test taking or study skills. On the other hand, if they're not doing their work or studying, regardless of what teachers are reporting to you in the form of grades, you should encourage your children to do more. You can expect children to become involved in the kinds of efforts that will permit you to recognize whether they're performing to their best ability.

Intelligent children should be brought up with the assumption that they'll be going on with post-high school education. Projected savings of money for college and assumptions that college follows high school are appropriate. Decisions for post-high school educational directions are among the most important ones that you and your children will make. It's even good that children talk about career goals early and often. Your part of the discussion should involve positive messages about effort and perseverance as they relate to college. You may also provide an atmosphere of flexibility and exploration relative to potential career and educational choices.

A case study example of the importance of college expectation follows:

> Rob and Joe, seventh graders, left science class together, talking as they walked. Both had received an *F* on their tests. Rob said to Joe, "I failed the test, again. I guess I'll drop out of high school and be a garbage collector." Joe didn't respond, but as an adult he remembered the conversation. At the time, he couldn't figure out why Rob wouldn't go on to college, nor why he thought that a failed test could make him a garbage collector. He had a similar failing grade and it had never occurred to him that he wouldn't go to college. All his friends and his family went to college. It followed naturally after high school graduation.

Although I don't know the comparable abilities of Rob and Joe, I do know that Rob dropped out of high school and Joe earned a Ph.D. No doubt there was more to the case than expectation, but their views of their futures, even from seventh grade, probably did have some effect on their accomplishments.

As a small child, college can be referred to as a matter-of-fact course of events that will be part of your children's education. By junior high school and early senior high school, more specific college directions can be given. For example, financial issues and specific career directions should begin to influence your children's thinking. If a state university is your intended direction, then the alternative levels of that education should be alluded to. For example, higher levels should be encouraged for those planning to do graduate work and the somewhat lesser challenge for those planning to complete only an undergraduate degree. By that time, you'll have a better sense of children's capabilities. Among very intelligent children, your most important criterion will be their motivation and interest. By senior high school, serious consideration of specific colleges should take place.

Obviously, college choices are difficult to make. How much of the decision belongs to adults and how much to adolescents is debatable and families take very different positions on college. If cost is an issue, parents shouldn't hesitate to state their own financial limitations and guidelines. Although scholarships and loans are available, the extent of indebtedness that young people may become involved in should be carefully discussed. Although education is a most important investment, you, as parents, shouldn't be expected to make major economic sacrifices in your own lives when less expensive quality alternatives are available. Many very good state universities seem more attractive to students from far away. They'll pay high tuition although the the university may not be appreciated by students within the home state. The proximity doesn't diminish the quality but often greatly reduces the cost. Living on campus usually permits sufficient independence. You, as parents, shouldn't assume that your children should be allowed to make a college decision entirely on their own. They deserve your guidance and advice although they may not acknowledge that.

Size of university is frequently an issue for decision making. However, it's a matter of personal preference rather than a matter of quality. If your child plans to pursue graduate education, a large university is more likely to provide undergraduate research experiences which will be helpful to entering graduate school. If your child is easily intimidated by large numbers, then the closeness of a small college may provide more support. Women's colleges have been reported to provide more leadership experiences for female students than coeducational schools. On the other hand, social interaction between the genders is more spontaneous at the latter.

Adjustment to college is frequently difficult, even for well-prepared, intelligent students. They may have a history of high school success which may be much more difficult to maintain at college. Preparations for that adjustment for you and your children are important. If grades aren't as high as you and they had hoped, don't assume that it's related to their lack of effort. Most important, your young adults should be alerted to the availability of support people at college should they require some help. They should be assured that getting help isn't an indication of failure, but a very typical part of college adjustment. It may be especially difficult for you to identify with the pressure your adult children feel at college if you've never gone to college yourself. Don't be too quick to assume that they're goofing off if they claim they're studying hard. On the other hand, if they're skipping classes you have very good reason to suspect that they need either help or commitment before you invest further monies into their higher education. Inset 4.1 has some reminders for parents relative to college plans.

INSET 4.1 — SETTING EXPECTATIONS FOR COLLEGE

1. If your child appears to have college-level ability, make the assumption early that college will be an automatic part of their education. If you have had a post-college education, you may also make the assumption that your children have the capacity to go beyond college. This won't become a pressure for them if they're good students. If they become accustomed to the idea that education is a long-term process, they won't be as likely to be tempted by short-term gratifications such as instant cars and expensive clothes.

2. Be sure that your message about college and careers is no less challenging for females than it is for males. The concept that girls should marry their education is outdated and inappropriate to our present recognition of the capabilities of females.

3. Don't assume that adolescents are in the position to make all college decisions. Certainly they should be an important part of the choice. The economic component of college is the one in which parents should take a most important advisory role. Young people don't have a great deal of financial experience by age 18 and may burden themselves with long-term debt for the sake of short-term peer status. You're much more experienced about finances. Don't hesitate to provide both financial advice and limits.

4. Discuss with your adolescent the expectations for adjustment that are typical for college students. If you've attended college yourself, that's quite easy. If you haven't, you and your children may want to talk with a college counselor. College students should be prepared to understand three important issues including (a) college competition, (b) the large time requirement for study and (c) the availability and the not unusual need for counseling help during college.

263

Setting Expectations by Referential Speaking

No parents like their children labeled negatively. They feel concerned that classification such as "emotionally disturbed" or "educationally retarded" may cause their children to feel stupid or dumb or inadequate. Yet, some parents unintentionally label their children directly. They may accidentally call them weird or strange or even dumb or stupid. All of us know that such labeling will also harm our children. When we catch ourselves, we feel frustrated and avoid repeating it in the future.

Another kind of labeling which is less direct and more harmful is accidentally perpetrated when adults talk to each other about children and within children's hearing. I've coined the term, "referential speaking," to describe this activity which takes place frequently between parents, among parents and other relatives, between parents and teachers and, yes, even among teachers. The description of children's activities, behaviors and misbehaviors as if the children were not listening, may cause serious problems for children. Lest you think that only unintelligent people speak "referentially," let me assure you that **all** parents, relatives and teachers speak referentially sometimes and that it's not a function of lack of intelligence. Referential speaking is spontaneous talk by persons who feel most comfortable with spontaneity. They may be busy and not have the time or opportunity to speak confidentially and thus describe children without thinking about the impact on those children.

Referential speaking is not all negative. Referential speaking about children can set intentional expectations which are positive and which can provide a sense of positive control for them. So, for example, if you say to your spouse, "I notice that Elizabeth's really persevering in her efforts, she's showing initiative and doing more than what's expected," if Elizabeth is listening to your conversation (even from the other room), she will be encouraged in her perseverance and effort. She can control these and they represent positive qualities.

What kinds of referential speaking are harmful? Referential speaking which depowers children because it makes them feel inadequate or incapable is **always** harmful. Referential speaking that empowers children to manipulate adults is also harmful. Here are some examples of harmful referential speaking:

Case 1

Amy comes to kindergarten screening with her mother. Her mother introduces Amy to the teacher who welcomes Amy to the classroom. Amy doesn't say anything. Her mother feels embarrassed. She explains in Amy's presense, "I'm sorry, Mrs. Smith, that Amy isn't saying hello, but Amy is very shy. She's always been very shy."

Amy has probably heard 2,000 times before she ever entered school about how shy she was. Mother explains because of her own discomfort at Amy's poor manners. She explains to a teacher, to another parent, to a friend or to a relative why Amy doesn't say hello. What Amy has learned is that she is shy. She thinks that her shyness makes it impossible for her to say hello. Amy assumes that she is biologically, organically, internally, intentionally, forever shy. Why would Amy expect to say hello?

How could we change that referential speaking? Mother could say to Dad or vice versa, "Did you notice how nicely Amy's manners are improving?" When Amy is introduced to the teacher, Mother could ignore Amy's not saying hello and, instead, permit Amy to get right to work. Soon, Amy would forget she was shy and learn that she could say, "Hello" just like other children. When a parent comes to our Clinic to see me about their shy child, I ask them to erase the word "shy" from their vocabulary. They find that within a few days or a few weeks their child learns reasonable manners upon greeting other people. We can't necessarily change the child's total personality nor do we want to, but we can easily teach him or her normal social behaviors. Even a quiet, sensitive child has the capability of learning appropriate manners and will learn them if he or she is not labeled "shy" by the important adults in the child's environment.

Case 2

Scott's parents are at a conference with his fourth-grade teacher. The teacher comments, "Scott seems to be disorganized." Scott's mother and father agree. They add, "He's disorganized at home. His desk is a mess. His room is a mess." The teacher joins in. "His locker's a mess at school, too."

Scott listens from the back of the classroom. As he hears the familiar tirade about his disorganization, Scott, too, feels organically, biologically disorganized. How does a child become organized if he's born disorganized?

Case 3

What about Brian? He's impossible! Yes, Brian is impossible. He hears it every time his dad is out of town. His mother tells his dad on the telephone how impossible Brian has been. When his dad's at home and walks in the door from work, the first message from his mom is that Brian's been impossible again. What Brian knows is that he's not only impossible, but his mom is powerless to discipline him or guide him. He continues to "walk" all over his mother.

How could that be changed? Skip the impossibility of his behavior. Concentrate on the techniques that channel and limit that behavior and referentially speak to Dad or Grandma about his positive and improved behaviors. "Dad, Brian's been terrific help while you're traveling!" "Grandma, Brian seems to be maturing. He seems to be outgrowing his babyish misbehavior."

Referential speaking has a great deal of impact on children. It truly labels them. If you use it positively, it has positive impact. If you use it negatively, it may have a terrible impact on your children, their attitude about learning and their self-confidence. When you see the positive, tell someone. When you see the negative, limit it or ignore it, but don't talk about it if your children are anywhere within 1,000 feet. They have an extraordinary homing-in sensitivity when they hear their name. Don't you remember how you tuned in when you heard your parents talk about you? The more you say, the more you'll see.

One more example from my own personal experience. While I was writing the section on referential speaking for my last book, I thought I'd better experiment with Sara. Sara is our youngest child and I was always in school or working when she was being brought up, so I tried most everything out on Sara. In this case, Sara didn't know about the experiment (although she does now) nor did my husband know. He was sitting across from me at the kitchen table in

conversation after our day at work. Sara was upstairs in her bedroom doing her homework. I knew that Sara could hear everything upstairs that we talked about in the kitchen. So as part of the conversation with my husband, I simply injected a little bit of intentional referential speaking. I said, "Sara's been working so hard lately. She's getting so much homework done." We continued our conversation. It wasn't ten minutes before Sara came downstairs, saying in haste, "I just came down for a quick drink of water. I'm going right back up to do my homework. I'm really getting a lot done." The experiment worked and I knew that our positive referential speaking inspired Sara's continued hard work that evening.

Try it. You can make a difference in a day by referentially speaking to an adult about your child. Just give a positive message about that child's efforts or behaviors. Make sure that you're honest and realistic. You'll find how powerful adult communication can be for inspiring positive expectations for your children. Please be conscious of your referential speaking, either positive or negative, because as our grandparents used to say, "Little pitchers have big ears." Your children are listening. Even when you close the doors, they hear through walls. When you think they are asleep, they seem to absorb your words. Parent walks afford exercise and privacy. Difficult discussions can be left for the outdoors or absolutely private places.

Intrinsic Learning

If your children are to become learners, they must experience the excitement of learning. While school learning can be related to winning and grades without distracting from the joy of intrinsic learning, if your children don't develop interests and enjoy noncompetitive learning, the likelihood of their being lifelong learners diminishes. Furthermore, the peer distractions and the psychological stresses that mount when children have not developed interests, distract from their mental health and their self-confidence.

How do you, as parents, inspire children to lifelong joyful learning? The way that is most effective is for you to take some time to become learners yourselves. Developing interests, pursuing your own areas of competence, sharing learning experiences with your children and valuing your spouse's learning experiences provide effective routes for modeling the intrinsic learning which will strengthen your own and your children's lives.

Some parents pursue particular hobbies their entire lives and become heavily involved in interest groups and associations. Other parents may flit from hobby to hobby or pursue one interest for a number of years and then channel their energies in a different direction. Still other parents may pursue half a dozen interests simultaneously and seem to thrive on quantity and variety. There is no one right way to pursue interests and learning. The absence of interests, however, models for your children an absence of the valuing of learning. Encourage your children to participate with peers in shared interests. These may be summer activities and camps or special enrichment opportunities during the year. However, your messages to encourage them will be diminished if their parents don't show interest in other-than-work activities. If your career is also your avocation, and certainly many careers provide the depth and breadth to be both vocation and avocation, then you will want to express and describe how your career provides not only for your livelihood, but for your interest in learning.

To face the challenge of parenting your children whether they be infants in your arms or teenagers taller than you, your communications about learning involve giving them appropriate power and praise, providing them with adult support in the form of a united front, teaching them the habits and routines that will help them to be efficient in producing effective schoolwork, and finally, and most important, expecting and modeling for them the joy of learning.

REFERENCES

Adderholt-Elliott, M. (1987). *Perfectionism: What's bad about being too good.* Minneapolis, MN: Free Spirit Publishing.

Davis, G.A., & Rimm, S.B. (1989, 1985). *Education of the gifted and talented* (2nd ed.). Englewood Cliffs, NJ: Prentice-Hall.

Erikson, E.H. (1963). *Childhood and society* (2nd ed.). New York, NY: Norton.

Fay, J. (1983). *Who says you're so great?* Evergreen, CO: Institute for Professional Development, Ltd.

Fay, J. (1988a). *Helicopters, drill sergeants & consultants.* Evergreen, CO: Cline/Fay Institute, Inc.

Fay, J. (1988b). *Tickets to success.* Evergreen, CO: Cline/Fay Institute, Inc.

Fay, J. (1989). Choices start early. *Love and Logic Journal, 4* (4).

Freud, S. (1959). *Collected papers.* New York, NY: Basic Books, *4,* 13-21.

Harnack, S. (1972). *Free to be you and me.* Ms. Foundation, Inc.

Hetherington, E.M., & Frankie, G. (1967). Effects of parental dominance, warmth and conflict on imitation in children. *Journal of Personality and Social Psychology, 6,* 119-125.

Jones, R.P. (1989, February 20). *Milwaukee Journal.*

Kohlberg, L., & Gilligan, C. (1971). *The adolescent as philosopher.* Daedalus, *100,* 1051-1086.

Lincoln, A. (1858, June 16). From his speech at the Republican State Convention in Springfield, Illinois.

Mischel, W., Shoda, Y., & Rodriguez, M.L. (1989, May). Delay of gratification in children. *Science, 244,* 933-938.

Mussen, P.H., & Rutherford, E. (1963). Parent-child relations and parental personality in relation to young children's sex-role preferences. *Child Development, 34,* 589-607.

Piaget, J. (1932). *The moral development of the child.* New York, NY: Harcourt Brace.

Rimm, S. (1986). *Underachievement syndrome: Causes and cures.* Watertown, WI: Apple Publishing Company.

Rimm, S. (1988, May/June). Popularity ends at grade 12! *Gifted Child Today. 11* (56), 42-44.

Rimm, S., & Lowe, B. (1988, Fall II). Family environments of underachieving gifted students. *Gifted Child Quarterly, 32* (4), 353-359.

Rimm, S., Cornale, M., Manos, R., & Behrend, J. (1989). *Guidebook-underachievement syndrome: Causes and cures.* Watertown, WI: Apple Publishing Company.

Wechsler, D. (1974). *The Wechsler intelligence scale for children-revised.* New York, NY: Psychological Corporation.

SUBJECT INDEX

About the Author

Dr. Sylvia Rimm directs Family Achievement Clinic where she works with children, their parents and their teachers to provide children with an environment where they enjoy learning and feel good about themselves. She has reversed underachievement for hundreds of bright children. Her experiences as a psychologist, educator and a parent of four children have fostered her realistic and practical approaches to parenting.

Dr. Rimm earned her doctoral degree in Educational Psychology from the University of Wisconsin-Madison. She has developed creativity and achievement motivation tests which have been used in thousands of schools in the U.S. She is a member of the Board of Directors of the National Association for Gifted Children and of the State of Wisconsin Psychology Examining Board. "How To Parent So Children Will Learn" is her fourth successful book related to her favorite topics: parenting, underachievement, creativity and giftedness.

Dr. Rimm speaks throughout the country to parents and teachers and on radio and TV call-in shows. When people read her books or hear her, their most frequent comment is, "Dr. Rimm has surely been in our home."

Complete this order form for additional books and cassettes tapes by Sylvia B. Rimm from:
Apple Publishing Company*
W6050 Apple Road
Watertown, WI 53094

BOOKS:

_____ How To Parent So Children Will Learn $15.00

_____ Underachievement Syndrome: 15.00
Causes and Cures

_____ Guidebook - Underachievement: 32.00
Syndrome Causes and Cures

_____ Education of the Gifted & Talented   37.00
by Gary A. Davis & Sylvia B. Rimm

TAPE SETS:

_____ How To Parent So Children Will Learn 25.00
(set of 3)

_____ Underachievement Syndrome: 50.00
Causes and Cures (set of 6)

_____ Educating Gifted Children (set of 2) 18.00

Total Amount_____

_____
Name

_____
Address

_____

_____
Telephone Number

*A subsidiary of Educational Assessment Service, Inc. Send for free catalog for
tests for underachievement and creativity.